A NEW ATLAS

FOR

ENGLISH SCHOOL EDUCATION

DEREK TURNER

Published by Derek Turner Associates

Copyright © Derek Turner 2007
All rights reserved.

ISBN 978-0-9556815-0-9

ACKNOWLEDGEMENTS

I owe a great debt of gratitude to friends and colleagues who have helped me in bringing this book to fruition.

Christine Ryan and Jane Gifford, both of whom as expert inspectors know a great deal about the realities of school education, encouraged me to believe that the project was worthwhile and made valuable suggestions.

James Mason, a former teaching colleague turned educational writer and many other things besides, provided encouragement and practical advice.

John Charnley, teacher, inspector, expert in information technology and connoisseur of many of the good things in life, provided incalculable help with almost every aspect of preparing the text for internet publication.

Finally, this book would not have been possible but for the hundreds of teachers and thousands of pupils who had to endure the trauma of the inspector in their classroom, and from whom comes any wisdom about school education that I may have acquired over four decades.

A New Atlas for English School Education

Contents

Introduction 1

Part 1: Past and Present 4
Chapter 1   The Educational Cul-de-sac 1965 - 2005 4
Chapter 2   Promising Paths 12
Chapter 3   Enduring Tracks and Roads 28
Chapter 4   Fellow Travellers 40
Chapter 5   Salient Features, Redundant Features 44

Part 2: The Future 52
Chapter 6   Prelude: What's in a Name? 52
Chapter 7   The Joient Curriculum 55
Chapter 8   Planning Individual Joients 62
Chapter 9   Curricular Development 69
Chapter 10   Organising the school 75
Chapter 11   Assessment and Recording 84
Chapter 12   Educational Superstructure 97
Chapter 13   Special Features 103

Part 3: Getting There 109
Chapter 14   Prelude: A Moses Moment 109
Chapter 15   Developing the Curricular Framework 111
Chapter 16   Re-training the Practitioners 116
Chapter 17   Managing the Transition 121

Part 4: Unmapped territory 124
Chapter 18   "Here be Dragons" 124
Chapter 19   Compulsory Schooling and Compulsory Education –
                            Redefining the Phases 127
Chapter 20   Who Pays? 132
Chapter 21   Fundamental and Desirable Elements in History ... 136

Conclusion 142

A New Atlas for English School Education

Introduction

The proposals contained in this project have been gestating for many years[1]. Recent developments, or rather the lack of significant developments, have only served to reinforce my belief that English education needs radical reform. The reason that this is a new Atlas or map of an existing world rather than a new world is that very little in education is ever genuinely new. The implications of new scientific knowledge and technical innovation are the only important exceptions. The world of education, like the real world, is largely unchanging. What are needed are a new way of looking at it and a new emphasis on features hitherto ignored or downplayed; in other words, a new map of what is already there but often hidden or under-emphasised, or a new projection that brings to the fore the features of the educational world that really matter.

The time may be ripe for this new Atlas to make some impact on those responsible for shaping education: government, schools and teachers. Governments – regardless of political persuasion – have become ever more frustrated and desperate, though not of course admitting as much, that successive reforms have had no lasting or substantial effect on what it pleases them to call 'standards', more

---

[1] The inspiration for the title, however, came from the Atlas mountains during a long and rather tedious trip through desert terrain on a coach tour of Morocco.

properly the overall quality of pupils' achievement. Schools and teachers in the maintained sector have no option but to do what the government dictates. They struggle, particularly in socially disadvantaged areas, to implement each new initiative but rarely make any headway with their less motivated pupils and, despite tremendous expenditure of time and nervous energy, fall short of the targets that government has imposed on them. There are a few notable exceptions to this gloomy picture. Some of these result from exceptional leadership by headteachers. Such heads overcome all the obstacles thrown in their way by current educational policy and practice. But because they are exceptional, no national system can be based on what they can do. A few other successful schools have had the skill or good fortune to be able to circumvent the obstacles and teach their pupils what they think is best for them in the way that they think best. Independent schools are a little better placed than state schools to do this, as parents rather than government are their paymasters. However, parents tend to be conservative and mistrustful of schools that attempt to innovate. Most independent schools are also circumscribed in what they can teach, or believe that they are, by national examination syllabuses, even though a few have begun to challenge the government and use alternative certification. 'Curricular review' often features in their school development plans but only exceptionally does it result in any radical change in what is taught, how it is taught and to whom. The learning that takes place in the few exceptional maintained and independent schools shows that radically different approaches will work and can motivate pupils of all ages, abilities and aptitudes.

The essence of the best approach, which will be systematically described in a later section, is to build up pupils' knowledge and understanding of the world primarily through completion of joint enterprises that require knowledge and skills drawn from a range of subjects. These enterprises are superficially similar to the concepts of 'topic', 'project' and 'coursework' that have been generally found wanting. In reality, however, they are fundamentally different in the way that pupils learn through them, and in the nature of the teaching that supports them. A brief description on its own of the joint enterprise approach will probably do little to persuade the doubters, probably at this stage the majority of readers, of the merits of the approach. A better appreciation of its value will, hopefully, become apparent through two short and partial histories of English school education during the past two generations, one summarising the failures, the blind alleys; the other pointing to promising paths that have not been widely explored. Some of the pervasive and persistent educational myths also need to be disposed of before a detailed explanation of the joint enterprise approach is provided.

There will be some who see what is proposed as a mirage; others may regard it as an admirable but hopelessly utopian vision of the future. The proposals are certainly and necessarily radical but some of them are already being considered in government circles. In same week that I drafted the proposals for a return to national sampling rather than national tests (see chapter 11), the head of the Qualifications and Curriculum Authority (QCA) came up with a similar idea. Good sense and reality are starting to return to educational thinking. This work is intended as a catalyst to speed the process.

This work concentrates on education during the compulsory school years up to age 16. However, the principles apply equally to education 16-18. Part 4 deals briefly with how they might apply to the education of students.

Part 1: Past and Present

Chapter 1

The Educational Cul-de-sac 1965 - 2005

Comprehensive education – new organisational initiatives – GCSE for all – lower achiever projects – inclusion – 'equal opportunity' and mixed ability teaching – National Curriculum and assessment – 'driving up standards' through National Literacy and Numeracy projects.

In order to remain sensibly short, this history has to be partial in the sense of incomplete. It is also partial in that it is openly biased, focusing on those educational changes and events that are relevant to my theme. Biased but not prejudiced. My training as a historian instils a respect for following where the evidence leads; my training as a school inspector determines that pre-conceived theories, however attractive and plausible, are no substitute for what actually works. As the previous sentence implies, one thread of this history is autobiographical: I draw heavily on what I have directly observed as working or failing and on hard evidence provided by former inspector colleagues. The other thread is drawn from public knowledge of educational development over the last forty years. I am assuming that my readers will be at least broadly familiar with these and will therefore refer to them without lengthy description or explanation. The public history is more prominent than the autobiography in this chapter; the reverse is true in the next.

The most salient features of this forty-year period are the many educational initiatives that petered out in political disillusionment and teacher frustration or gloom. Not so much a single cul-de-sac as a series of blind alleys, some of them connected to each other but none leading with anything more than initial and minimal success towards the Holy Grail of educational improvement. What these initiatives had in common, apart from their eventual failure, was the diversion of the time and energy of politicians and, more importantly, schools and teachers away from the thinking about and implementing the essential components of teaching and learning.

The first, most influential and most pervasive initiative was the long drawn out and incomplete move to comprehensive education. This consumed vast resources of money as well as time and effort. Its social engineering aims were doomed to failure because there was no way that politicians could ensure that all geographical areas became equally socially advantaged. Consequently, comprehensives whose pupils came from leafy suburbs tended to thrive while those in downtrodden inner cities floundered. As it became apparent that comprehensives did not work, governments looked around for other forms of school organisation of a kind that matched their political ideologies. So the Conservatives came up with Grant Maintained and City Technology Colleges. Labour tried Foundation, Specialist Schools, and City Academies amongst others. Sometimes these organisations were in effect a reversal of the policies of the previous administration. These changes were predicated on one of two dogmas: either that giving schools financial autonomy would improve the overall quality; or that widening parental choice would force all schools to improve. Neither dogma is true so none of the initiatives were more than a partial success. Some schools, usually those already in favoured areas, profited and thrived on these initiatives; others proportionately declined, leaving the overall situation pretty much as before and the least academically motivated pupils as uninterested in their education as ever.

As disillusionment grew about the efficacy of structural reorganisation and change of status or control, politicians set off down another road in the quest for improvement, namely schools' public accountability for achieving quality measured through national tests and examinations for all, and through 'league tables'. Illogically, politicians started at the wrong end of this road, prescribing the examinations to be taken by all 16-year-olds before properly reviewing the curriculum for any school age group, including that for 14-16 year olds, or setting up a single examining body. The result was a mess, with GCSE boards competing for market share, a proliferation of GCSE syllabuses that allowed the canny schools to 'cherry pick' the syllabuses and control – some might say fix – their entry policies in ways that maximised their league table positions. Producing a single examination that suited pupils of all abilities proved impossible in some subjects. As a result, many syllabuses had to be re-written to include different tiers. The re-training of teachers for GCSE, the production and revision of an excessive number of syllabuses and the burgeoning examination bureaucracy soaked up much energy and intellectual capital. Not without some success perhaps. Examination results steadily improved, but universities and business were unconvinced and regularly complained of 'declining standards'. Young people did not appear to emerge from their schooling any better educated despite achieving better grades. And even in the official statistics the performance of the lowest achieving groups, including certain ethnic minorities, remained stubbornly low.

The problem of the hard core of underachievers led to the exploration of two other routes. The first, which pre-dated GCSE and ran counter to its philosophy of 'one exam fits all', had many variations such as the Lower Achiever Project and Vocational Education. Both of these projects, with laudable intent, set out to motivate the 'hard core' and get them to learn something useful. They largely failed on both counts. On the rare occasions that hard-core pupils were motivated, what they learnt was nearly always of minimal value, as (in the eyes of employers) were the certificates and diplomas that some of them eventually achieved. Educationalists and teachers poured extensive amounts of time and intellectual dedication, if not always much common sense, into these projects.

Quasi-public bodies, such as the Business and Technology Education Council (BTEC), were expensively staffed to devise or validate the syllabuses and to accredit the pupils' results. All with very little return for the investment.[1]

The second route, mapped out at the height of the political correctness era, was 'inclusion'. Again, the motives behind the many special projects and initiatives were excellent, as individually were some of the projects, but their proliferation and the need for the schools to jump through separate bureaucratic hoops for each of them tied up yet more teacher time and expertise. Once again, the already thriving schools tended to be more successful in gaining additional funding. The more needy were not always so successful; and even success with a particular project threatened to fragment the school and its curriculum. Inclusion projects did not in the end provide any great leap forward.

Of all the primrose paths to educational wellbeing the most inviting to politicians, schools and teachers alike was signposted 'equal opportunity'. Never, in terms of what this aspiration actually produced, was a phrase so misleading; but its seductiveness fooled some of the best educational minds for a generation, wasted millions of pounds and crucially diverted attention away from the essence of good education. Far too many examples abound to expose them all. Amongst the madding crowd, the decimation of special schools in the name of 'integration' blighted the education of the already disadvantaged while placing intolerable strains on teachers who lacked the time or specialist training to cope. Lady Warnock, rarely amongst politicians and experts, has at least acknowledged that she got it wrong. It is less easy to pin the blame on any individual for the great mixed-ability teaching fiasco, an unnecessary by-product of 'going comprehensive' that spawned tens of thousands of worthless

---

[1] This is not intended as a general criticism of BTEC, which for a long time has carried out the valuable task of testing the competence of those engaged on vocational training. BTEC's contribution to school education has, however, been of limited worth.

worksheets, bemused slow learners, bored and frustrated fast learners and created mountainous overloads of work for hard-pressed teachers. When linked, as in some primary schools, to the absurd concept of the 'integrated day', teachers of ten-year-olds might be found not only coping with pupils of greatly varying abilities but also trying to teach up to four different subjects at once![2]

The absurdities and waste of intellectual effort resulting from the dogma of mixed ability gradually became apparent to all but its most blinkered and fundamentalist disciples. Government, too, finally came to realise that something had to be done about the curricular anarchy of the late 1980s if serious progress was to be made in English education. Thus was born the National Curriculum, as legend has it on the back of an envelope by Margaret Thatcher and restricted to the 'basics'. Had it been restricted to language and number, and the vast resources that were actually frittered away by endless working parties and their offshoots concentrated on these, it might indeed have created something of a breakthrough. However, in the hands of the government bureaucrats and armies of 'experts' drawn from educational research establishments, the National Curriculum became a 'white mammoth' occupying more time in the curriculum than was actually available without unproductive rushing through the syllabuses. Soon after it was created and introduced into schools, it had to be cut down to manageable elephantine size. Also despite its bulk, it failed to encompass all that pupils needed to learn. So extra 'limbs' such as 'citizenship' were grafted on and other subject areas such as religious, personal, health and social education more loosely attached. This lumbering committee-bred outsize animal cost a fortune in resources of all kinds. But, while it brought a degree of conformity to the curricular anarchy, it did little either to improve the lot of the hard core of underachievers or to provide an

---

[2] This is no exaggeration. I observed this happening in a school full of good but ideologically misguided teachers, who expended prodigious amounts of effort in planning and carrying out fiendishly complicated lesson plans to very little effect.

educational system that was 'fit for purpose' in the 21st century. The most recently announced curricular review is little more than a re-design of this clumsy beast. Its progenitors have realised some of the problems but done little that will improve its usefulness.

There are two main reasons for this lack of fitness, and an appreciation of these are crucial to my joint enterprise proposals. Firstly, even if the National Elephant had been evolved as a sleek panther it would not have fitted current educational needs because it was conceived as a conglomeration of academic subjects. Government's insistence on defining the curriculum in terms of subjects was a seriously retrograde step running contrary to the promising developments that preceded it. This theme will be taken up in greater detail in a later chapter. The second reason for lack of fitness relates to the vast assessment superstructure that was laid over the National Curriculum. Every part of the elephant was to be elaborately and minutely measured, from ever earlier years to age 14, at which point the whole centralised Rolls Royce of a system was prevented from being extended to age 16 so that the, by now, ageing and cobbled-together GCSE charabanc to continue its polluting way.

I find it very difficult to retain my historian's and inspector's objectivity in face of the assessment frenzy, having been far too closely involved in the whole process, and I still find it obscene that millions of pounds were spent developing the original national tests that were patently from the start far too elaborate ever to be a practical proposition in schools. I still remain angry at the ludicrous demands made initially of 'teacher assessment' and moved by the plight of the salt-of-earth primary teacher reduced to tears in the presence of a visiting inspector by the seeming mountain of tests and reams of forms she felt unable to cope with. The assessment frenzy not only wasted millions; it also, perhaps more than any of the other blind alley initiatives, sapped teachers' confidence and reduced their morale. And to what end? After the usual initial improvement, at least in the raw test results, the figures flattened out and are in danger of drifting down. Some age-related tests have been abandoned, others played down. The Rolls Royce has gone rusty, and had government been able to bring itself to do it, would be heading for the breaker's yard. All that it has actually done is to strip out those parts which are most blatantly broken while failing to appreciate the fundamental problems of the system itself.

The last major initiative of the period: 'driving up standards' – as defined by test and examination results - looked initially promising in that it focused on disseminating good teaching practice. Some credit must be given to those involved in the National Literacy and Numeracy Projects. Statistical gains were achieved, at least in terms of 'standards' as defined, but the inevitable effects of a 'one-style fits all' approach to teaching, as represented by the literacy and numeracy hours, were counter-productive for all but the middling majority. As with mixed ability, the slower learners were starved of sufficient attention; the quicker learners held back. More importantly, the notion that 'raising standards' was the be-all and end-all of education, led schools to operate in ways that made them publicly successful but in reality less effective, primarily because of the poor match between 'standards' and genuine educational achievement. Some pupils' choice of subjects became determined more by the likelihood of a high grade than by its educational usefulness and relevance. Rare indeed was the reaction of one chairman of governors when informed of the school's best-ever results – "oh no, that means next year, if the results go down, all the parents will be moaning about declining standards!" Once again, success, as measured by tests and examinations, was short and limited.

The moral of this sad story is clear. Constant changes of government policy, a plethora of new initiatives, ever-increasing bureaucracy and a misguided adherence to a notion of equal opportunity, all drained the educational exchequer and the energy of teachers and distracted educational researchers and teacher training institutions from getting to grips with what really needed to be done. In short, forty wasted years. Or nearly wasted. Despite the exhausting and dispiriting effects of discovering so many much vaunted routes turn into blind alleys, here and there far-sighted teachers and perceptive educationalists did make a start down the right paths, particularly during the first half of the period before the obsession with 'driving up standards' largely suppressed all worthwhile activities. The story of these 'promising paths' is taken up in the next chapter.

Chapter 2

Promising Paths

Refighting Naseby – hunting buffalo – manufacturing folders – solving the circulation problems and sorting the engine – Mary Rose, Valley of the Kings, police station and newsroom – mixed-age tasks – TVEI – ROA

The previous chapter was depressing to write, charting as it did the educational failures and blind alleys over a period that roughly coincided with my professional involvement in education as teacher and inspector. I have to confess that, like others, I too was misled into believing that some of the initiatives would lead to sustained progress. The GCSE was one such. Seduced by the socialist attractiveness of a single examination for all I suppressed for too long my doubts about the practicality of the concept. However, I realised the hopelessness of most of the new initiatives while they were still proposals and being proved right again and again provided only a bitter kind of satisfaction. Had this catalogue of unfulfilled hopes been the whole educational story, I would probably have deserted education long before I did. Fortunately, behind the headline failures were episodes of genuine success. These provided hope and renewed commitment. Even so, they brought their own frustrations. Many of the promising paths were not followed up sufficiently to become a feature on the educational map. Some that did become well known were deliberately blocked by government and their funding diverted to financing one of the blind alleys. It is these, now neglected or blocked paths, that form the substance of this chapter. Because few were ever part of national policy and most were due to initiatives by individual schools, even individual teachers, this chapter is something of a rag-bag of diverse practices without any obvious or immediate connections. The following chapter, however, brings them into some kind of order as salient features that can be expected to be present in the new educational Atlas. Part 2 considers the various pages of the Atlas in greater detail.

The first scrap from the ragbag is purely anecdotal, autobiographical and pre-dates the start of the period under review. It derives from my very first experience of teaching: a few 'taster' weeks with a small number of post-scholarship boys in a prep school during the summer term. Nothing deriving from such a privileged position within a privileged institution could ever qualify as blueprint for a national system of education, but for me it provided the first small ascent up the long learning curve of what constitutes good education. The project that I and the boys undertook was concerned with researching the battle of Naseby – close to the school – from the near-contemporary account by Clarendon and then re-enacting the battle on the ground as best as could be achieved by half a dozen people. (Naturally, given the social origins of the boys, we took only the Royalist side!) The lessons that I learnt from what proved a successful project, apart from confirming that I did want to devote my life to teaching, were firstly that pre-teen and teenage pupils like nothing better than actually doing things; secondly that, given the prospect of doing something, they will grapple with reading and coming to understand demanding books; thirdly that in the course of doing things they are ready to be guided by the teacher and keen, in the light of this guidance, to contribute their own individual and group ideas and make group decisions. (Faced with the reality of the 20th century Leicestershire countryside, neither Clarendon's description, nor my historian's training provided anything like a complete answer to who charged where and when.) Finally, the project, more through good fortune than any planning of mine, demonstrated that what motivated 13-year-olds – and any age-group from about four upwards – is the combination of individual 'research' and joint action in successfully completing an enterprise. Whether the historical learning on this occasion was factually correct is dubious: scholars still argue about the details of the battle. The true learning lay in all the incidentals, the gathering of evidence, the debate, the decisions, the co-operation and the subject-specific understanding that 'historical truth' is slippery and hard to come by.

I will make no further references to my own teaching failures and successes. This is not an ego trip nor is it primarily about historical learning. I will, therefore, jump some 20 years in time to my early years as an inspector. The next two vignettes are both from history lessons observed, but it is not primarily the historical learning that is important here.

The first vignette is a double period of Year 7 history in a Fenland comprehensive, a young teacher willing to step out of line and a mixed-ability group, some of whom are lacking enthusiasm or willingness to exercise their brains or challenge their stereotyped views. The general topic is Early Man and the particular topic the hunting of buffalo. The teacher, with some success, is getting the class to discuss why 'progress' away from hunter/gathering to farming was slow. One of the bored boys, in a brief moment of what for him is active involvement, says that progress was slow because 'cos they were all stoopid'. (No doubt, being a Fenlander he is a dab hand at ploughing a straight furrow.) The teacher, having presumably anticipated some such remark and made prior arrangements with the head of PE, said "Right, we're going to spend the next part of this lesson trying to hunt buffalo. Down to the gym, collect some javelins and a vaulting horse; put the horse on the playing field, pretend it is a buffalo and we'll see how well we do." (Nowadays, of course, the Health and Safety folk would faint with horror at such a prospect.) After twenty minutes or so of trying, not a single pupil managed to wing the – stationary – vaulting horse even from rather closer than a hunter was ever likely to be to a moving buffalo. Back to the classroom; grudging admission from the bored boy that Early Man was not so 'stoopid' after all, and a general appreciation by the class that 'primitive' does not mean 'stupid', whether palaeolithic man or modern Amazonian tribes. A useful piece of historical learning but even more valuable as part of personal and social education. The fact that health and safety requirements would now make it impossible to replicate the details of the lesson in the 21st century is unimportant. The important features are the need, as often as practicable, to learn through doing, and the value of direct, even if proxy, experience.

The second vignette, from the same era, is another double period, this time of humanities with a historical theme. A mixed-ability Year 9 class in brand-new school in a Fenland edge 'raw' new town, full of socially deprived and recently uprooted families. The broad topic is the Industrial Revolution; the particular topic the factory system and the advantages of specialisation of labour. The teacher is a gifted head of humanities who wants to get away from the dreary litany of inventions (which nearly always took decades anyway to make any social or economic impact) and concentrate on the impact of the factory system. The introductory lesson for this topic involved a series of teams 'manufacturing' folders. Some teams had to undertake the whole process; others were specialists: folding, cutting out, glueing, quality control and so on. The teams were of mixed ability and all started with no knowledge of how to make a folder. After initial explanation of the process by the teacher, the groups set to work. No surprise that the productivity of the 'specialist' groups' rapidly increased and soon far outpaced the generalist groups. When the 'factory' closed, the teacher re-assured the somewhat crestfallen generalist groups that their low productivity was not their fault. During the work, various glitches in the specialist group production line that slowed productivity (inaccurate folding, too little glue etc.) emerged and pupils needed little prompting from the teacher to appreciate the importance of keeping the production line moving. The 'specialists' also quickly realised the tedium of being just a gluer or a folder – and perhaps came to empathise with what many of their parents were doing all day. This short simulation provided a 'real-life' introduction to 18th century textile factories that increased pupils' understanding of the factors involved and their motivation to find out about the Yorkshire and Lancashire mills. Though the lesson was overtly historical it also gave pupils an experiential insight into social and economic factors independent of a particular era or place and was thus an all too rare example of good humanities learning. In the context of an even less restrictive school curriculum it could have easily been extended to include several other 'subject' elements such as folder design, marketing; and even, given current concerns, recycling. (In fact, the head of humanities, being devious in the best possible way, had decided on making folders so that they could then be used by other pupils for future projects: cost-effective recycling ahead of its time.)

Where classes consisted wholly or largely of the 'hard core' of poorly motivated pupils, it was rare for teachers to generate successful learning. However, amongst the long list of failed endeavours, there were some successes. The next vignette is one of them.

Time has moved on since the previous vignettes but GCSE and the National Curriculum are still to come. The South Midlands comprehensive is in a socially average area but most of the brighter pupils are siphoned off into the several independent schools in the neighbourhood and it has at least its fair share of the normally underachieving and under-motivated. The school has identified these pupils and treats them as a separate group. The buildings, relevant to this story, are seventies brutal, with long narrow corridors and stairways making movement round the school difficult and contributing to the amount of pushing and shoving that is part of a male teenager's way of life. When I arrive as the inspector looking specifically at the provision made for the low achievers, I am surprised and delighted to discover that instead of the usual, at best, grudging co-operation and, at worst, truanting, this group is full of pride in its achievements. From the pupils themselves, with some additional details provided by the teacher in charge of the group, I discover why. They have just been publicly commended and thanked in assembly by the head for their work, which has been to the benefit of the whole school. In an inspired moment, the teacher in charge suggested to the senior management team (SMT) that his group should be allowed to look at the circulation problem within the school and try to come up with a solution. Though the teacher is far too professional to say so explicitly, I get the impression that the SMT, which has grappled with the problem itself without success, agrees to this idea only to humour him and to give the group something useful to do. To the surprise of many, though not the teacher or the pupils themselves, they tackle this challenge with enthusiasm and dedication. Furthermore they come up with a circulation plan that looks distinctly promising. The school gives it a trial and it works well. It is permanently adopted. The group has its 'fifteen minutes of fame' in assembly. More importantly, the confidence in themselves of its members and consequently in their willingness and ability to learn is given an enormous boost. Though I do not witness the process at first hand, talking with the pupils convinces me that this was a genuine group achievement. The teacher contributed to the discussions but the greater part of the work and the decisions were the pupils'. This story again illustrates the value as a motivator of a group enterprise and, in this instance, a genuine real-life problem. Even more importantly, it demonstrates the point that intelligence cannot be measured on a linear scale but that there are multiple intelligences best measured as a profile rather than single score or grade. This is well known to psychologists but a fact widely forgotten or ignored by those with responsibility for educating the young.

(The fact that psychologists are divided about whether the concept of 'general intelligence' is a reality is irrelevant here. Some argue that non-intellectual skills, such as entrepreneurial 'know how' are not aspects of intelligence. However, whether or not intelligence is single and general or specialist and multiple, it is self-evident that different humans have the capacity to excel in different ways. This is not to argue that all humans are equally good at something; it is equally self-evident that some individuals excel in a wide variety of ways and that others have little capacity for anything. Between these extremes, however, most have some potential skills in at least one area. It is one of the purposes of education to identify these, to foster and value them. Whether or not, for example, highly skilled footballers should be described as intelligent is largely a matter of semantics and debate by philosophers and psychologists.)

In the same vein is the possibly apocryphal but very plausible – if sexist – anecdote of the two female school inspectors on their way to inspect a comprehensive. Their car breaks down and as they are gazing somewhat mournfully at the engine, having succeeded at least in raising the bonnet, a teenager cycles up and asks them if they need any help. They explain their problem and he looks at the engine, tinkers with it a bit and soon has it going again. The two inspectors thank him warmly, but being inspectors, can't help but wonder why he is not at school, nor can they resist asking him. "Oh" says he "I do normally go to school, but they told me and the other thickies to stay away today because the inspectors are coming."

All these vignettes, apart from my teaching taster experience, have been drawn from the secondary phase, but promising paths were also being developed in primary schools, more frequently because of the greater curricular freedom they enjoyed until the dead hand of the National Curriculum and tests brought most pioneering work to an end. The arrival of computers in primary schools in the late seventies and early eighties brought about a sudden spurt in educational innovation. The computer was the spur and the catalyst in making certain things easy or possible that would have been difficult or impossible before. But in the longer term it was not the computer itself but the fact that it caused perceptive educationalists and classroom teachers to come up with exciting new approaches that marked genuine progress; nowhere more so than in a clutch of primary schools in East Anglia, whose heads had joined themselves into an organisation to promote the use of computers in primary schools. It is probably better to sketch the range of projects rather than describe just one in detail. Capitalising on the publicity afforded to the raising of the Mary Rose, one involved first using the computer to locate the wreck in the Solent and then search for, bring up and try to identify the 'finds'. In addition to developing computing skills that were at that stage unfamiliar, pupils also had to learn mapping skills in three dimensions and a mix of archaeological and historical skills in trying to identify their finds. The project involved both group and individual work and because access to the computer was limited – they were still expensive for schools to buy – they also had to learn how to organise themselves in a way that made best use of the machine.

A rather similar project involved searching for finds in the Egyptian Valley of the Kings. However, additional skills were required. Pupils had to write letters to the 'Egyptian Department of Antiquities' to get permission to undertake their excavations. This involved working out a plan and then trying to justify the undertaking to the authorities. The 'Department' would not grant permission until a workable plan was devised and the letter was clearly and persuasively written. Financial and resource factors were also involved. Pupils had a limited budget and resources, of transport, fuel and workers for instance, so they had to work out what they could afford and how best to deploy their resources.

A third project moved right away from history and geography to the contemporary world. In what was a tiny school, one of the two classrooms was rigged up as a police station. Pupils had to run the station, deal with incoming calls and information. They had to develop skills of dealing with conflicting evidence, information overload, making quick decisions and so on. Similar to this, though in Year 7 of a secondary modern school in a different area, was a simulated news-room where all kinds of confused, incomplete and contradictory reports had to be analysed, evaluated and ultimately turned into 'copy'. This last example produced some of the most highly motivated and sophisticated activity by pupils deemed by the 11 plus to be less able that I had observed with any pupils of similar age. All these projects shared many of the features of those described in earlier vignettes. What particularly characterised them, however, was the tremendous enthusiasm that they generated, which in turn speeded up the effective learning of skills. There was also an element of competition between the groups: who got the most finds etc.

Encouraging competition in children's education tends to be frowned upon by left-leaning educationalists and, as with most things, if indulged in excessively, harms rather than fosters personal and social development. Building into such projects or joint enterprises a modest element of competition is, however, desirable, not only to increase motivation but also to develop the ability to win, and lose, gracefully.

One, more recent, vignette before looking at the better known promising paths. This is from the very recent past and, partly because of the odds against finding anything original and illuminating within the state sector in recent years for the reasons given in the previous chapter, this comes from an independent girls' primary school in the East Midlands. This school contains a well above average proportion of able and highly motivated pupils. Unsurprisingly therefore it achieves excellent national test results. Some such schools are content to rest on these national test laurels, but the teachers here were aware that there was still scope for higher educational achievement, particularly amongst those they judged to be the most able. They therefore instituted a special 'gifted and talented' programme of tasks and activities that took place every second week, replacing the normal timetable during one afternoon. It had succeeded so well that the school decided to see whether it would also work with those not designated as gifted or talented. It was at this point that I and my co-inspectors observed it and were amazed by the extremely high level of achievement, the pace of learning and the nature of the work undertaken. Pupils mainly worked in groups of about four to six, though some of the tasks were individual. The tasks varied widely, across and well beyond the traditional primary curriculum. Most involved inter-disciplinary knowledge and skills. One task, for example, was reminiscent of 'the Great Egg Race', building as high and stable a tower as possible out of distinctly unpromising materials and requiring considerable 'lateral thinking' to get anything to stand up at all. Another was, in effect, a controlled experiment by which pupils discovered which style of learning suited them best. Undertaken by first-year university students it would have been called psychology of learning and the level of learning achieved would not have disgraced such students.[1] All the projects were meticulously planned by the team of teachers involved but once the tasks were explained, their role was largely restricted to facilitating, monitoring what pupils were doing, timekeeping and conducting the debrief towards the end of the lesson. Perhaps the most striking feature of this highly successful approach was the composition of the groups. All the classes from age 8 to age 11 were regrouped into mixed-age classes. The pupils were faced with working to tight deadlines with people they did not know well. It was fascinating to watch how the social dynamics of the groups developed, how efficiently most of the groups worked together and how, in some groups, it was the eight-year-old who took the lead and was quickly accepted by her older peers as leader.

This story demonstrates that such purposeful joint enterprises can raise the levels of the most academically able pupils to unexpected heights just as they can for the less academically endowed. This is an important point, because it is sometimes argued that 'traditional', 'chalk and talk' teaching methods are the best for academically bright pupils. Certainly they can thrive on such an approach, as indeed they can on any approach that challenges them. This vignette, however, suggests that a 'non-traditional' approach works even better. Even those groups who did not do so well in achieving the task, whose towers toppled, clearly learnt rapidly and effectively from their errors. This example also challenges the assumption, made by the vast majority of English schools and educationalists, that pupils should be grouped by age. Learning in year groups is shown not to be a necessary, perhaps not even the most desirable, condition of

---

[1] Shortly after drafting this, a very similar lesson was featured in a TV programme about intelligence, this time featuring a class of younger secondary pupils of unstated ability in a maintained school.

successful learning. Learning to accept the notion of younger people as team leaders or managers, a commonplace in the world of work, proved useful personal and social lessons for the pupils, and perhaps for the teachers too!

And now to the better known promising paths, trackways rather, that were prematurely terminated. The first is the Technical and Vocational Education Initiative (TVEI). As originally devised this was a rather crude vocational scheme mainly provided, as usual, for those deemed academically less able. However, some of the schools involved in the project developed it into a much more sophisticated system involving most if not all the ability range and a fruitful marrying of subject areas. Unfortunately for me, I was never involved directly in inspecting this initiative and cannot therefore vouch for its effectiveness first-hand. However, colleagues who did inspect it grew in enthusiasm for what it achieved, while acknowledging their initial difficulty as teams of subject specialist inspectors in evaluating a course that repeatedly crossed subject boundaries. (Even more than usual, the inspectors were learning from what they saw as well as providing feedback.) One of TVEI's chief features was enabling pupils to see the direct links between what they were learning and the 'world of work' and the relevance and value of the so-called 'life skills' that they were developing. It was initially successful because it was relatively well funded at the start and therefore well resourced even though the curriculum thinking was initially crude. It continued to be successful, even when funding dwindled, because schools were allowed to evolve the scheme in the light of their own experiences or the experiences of others mediated through well-qualified TVEI advisers, who were able to pass on best practice. It only foundered because it fell foul of the 'one curriculum for all mantra' described in the previous chapter.

A similar fate befell what was probably the best example of grass roots initiative and government co-operation, the Records of Achievement pilot scheme (ROA). I was deeply involved in monitoring this project, initially sceptical and ultimately, faced with abundant evidence of good practice, persuaded of its genuine and lasting merits as a way forward. The story of ROA is a classic tragedy in the Greek tradition provided that one counts the fickleness of government as the fatal flaw, but this is the optimistic chapter so it is not the last-minute barring of the ROA way by government to make room for the National Curriculum highway – though they could have co-existed – that concerns us here. Rather it is the many positive features of the ROA initiative itself and the way it was developed that it is important to appreciate. It can still serve as a useful model for both.

Taking the mode of development first, ROA was rare, perhaps unique, in being a grass roots initiative taken up and supported by a government that, remarkable as it now seems, did not try to direct its development from on high but encouraged a genuine partnership approach. And what a partnership, with representatives from schools, 'lefty liberal' organisations, examination boards, university education and research departments, business, industry and local education authorities. The role of central government was restricted to pump-priming finance so that the various authorities could fund local projects, and to general monitoring of the developments nationally by professional educationalists, that is inspectors, rather than civil servants, politicians or 'special advisers'. The civil servants were kept in the picture but trusted the messages that the inspectors were relaying to them. Happy days! The considerable diversity of the steering group representation initially seemed a most unpromising mixture, ranging as it did from those who started from the belief that judging children in any way was inherently wrong to the hard-line examination boards for whom anything other than academic qualifications were a waste of time, or equally hard-line business people concerned with basic skills, reliability and punctuality. Yet as the various local education authority projects developed, with their different emphases, strengths and weaknesses, a remarkable meeting of minds and adjustment of positions took place. The unpromising mixture became a stable compound, producing a final report with recommendations that all groups felt able to support. Meanwhile, the projects themselves and the schools within them nearly all flourished. Because it was a bottom-up enterprise with scope for experimentation within sensible limits, and also because the mainly high-quality project leaders were given the opportunity to meet and exchange experience and expertise, there was a strong commitment to making sure the initiative was a success. Originally focused on the 11-16 age group, ROA was starting to spread both up and down the age-range before the way was abruptly blocked.

The outcomes and process of ROA pioneered ways forward in assessment that still point to a fair and valuable way of judging and recording achievement. In considering what constituted achievement, ROA spread its net widely. Success in tests and examinations was given its due weight, but placed alongside other undoubted and not necessarily precisely quantifiable achievements. These included all kinds of extra-curricular, sporting and outdoor education achievements, contributions to the local community, and proto-business achievements from the humble paper-round to full-scale enterprises. Furthermore, following the philosophy of the excellent Hargreaves Report[2] presented to the ILEA, pupils' positive attitudes to work, as evidenced in their commitment, regular and punctual attendance and meeting of deadlines, were also treated as achievements in their own right.

Two crucial elements of the process were pupils' self-assessment and external validation of achievement. The completion of the physical record of the ROA was not a one-off, short-term affair. The process of externally validated self-assessment lasted for at least three

---

[2] It is one of the lesser tragedies of 20th century education that David Hargreaves's report to the ILEA was never effective, despite the fact that its author became, as an inspirational Chief Inspector for ILEA, the person charged with implementing his own recommendations. Sadly, the futilities of the unrelenting political ideologies rampant at the time combined with ILEA's ludicrously bureaucratic approach to management and governance, prevented even the highly gifted team of ILEA inspectors from making any real headway in implementing the report.

years, and for five in some schools. Pupils were required to make their own decisions from the start about what their achievements were and how well they had done. In the early stages their judgements were naturally often crude or simplistic but through teacher guidance and growing experience became increasingly sophisticated and valid. An essential feature of the process was that pupils were not just required to make judgements about their achievements but also to learn how to express these clearly orally and on paper in what amounted to a rolling and evolving curriculum vitae. Some of the minor achievements of earlier years were pruned and replaced with those of more substance couched in more sophisticated language. But this process was not a free ride for the self-deluded or the over-optimistic. All achievements and acquired skills had to be validated: by the school staff, temporary employers, the heads of community homes, the elderly whose gardens were kept tidy, the local business people who judged the enterprises, the sports coaches and the outdoor education instructors.

A particular strength of this multi-faceted achievement profile was that the various kinds of achievement were not hierarchically ordered. Individual pupils, the school, and potential employers were all able to order their own priorities as suited their needs or beliefs. Potential employers and further education gatekeepers, for instance, would be likely to give different weightings to particular areas of achievement. From the point of view of pupils intellectually incapable of more than modest academic examination achievements, ROA was a godsend that allowed them to highlight their equally valid and worthwhile capabilities and attitudes. As with the 'fifteen minutes of fame' in assembly described earlier in the chapter, the fact than non-academic achievements could be included and highly rated proved a powerful boost to the confidence of those gifted in ways other than doing well in examinations. This confidence, in turn, tended to raise their overall level of achievement, even sometimes in their weaker areas.

During the life of the ROA pilot there was keen debate about whether the record should be wholly positive or also record failures.

Supporters of the latter approach argued, with some justification, that the ROA document could end up as no more than what in a later decade would have been called a great deal of spin on threadbare substance. Ultimately, the positives only group carried the day, and rightly, because experience showed that it was easy enough to infer from the thinness and modest levels of the recorded achievements in some ROA what were the weaknesses and failures of these pupils.

One of the keys to the success of the ROA pilot was the realisation that the process and the outcomes were inextricably linked, and that both were essential to its success, a point incidentally that government failed to appreciate when it belatedly re-introduced an emasculated version that operated only in the last two compulsory years and was overbalanced in favour of the final product. This neutered version gave ROA a bad name and ensured that it did not long survive.

In the original pilot, the importance of having a 'piece of paper' at the end of the process that would be valued by employers was always a key point. For this reason, schools in the pilot worked hard to 'sell' the ROA product to local businesses and colleges, not just by producing a well-presented document but also by involving them from an early stage in advising on what it should contain and what it should look like. Schools usually made quite an occasion of the annual presentation of ROAs, often graced by local worthies and notables as well as governors and parents. While some might regard this as a case of the Dodo's Caucus race in *Alice in Wonderland* where everyone won and received a prize, the school leavers mainly rated the occasion and the ROA itself highly.

In case this necessarily brief account suggests that all was perfect, there were of course difficulties. For example, further education admission tutors and potential employers wanted leavers to bring their ROAs with them when they attended interviews, usually in the spring term, or to send them with their applications, but at that stage they were incomplete, particularly because the examination results were, unavoidably, missing. However, such difficulties were not insuperable and did not detract from the almost universal welcome that the scheme received. (The teachers' unions moaned a little about the extra workload on teachers involved; little did they know what was to come a few years later!)

Chapter 3

Enduring Tracks and Roads

Telford CTC – Early Years education

So far, the Atlas shows a considerable number of ambitious education highways that peter out into nothing – rather like the EU-funded, short stretches of dual carriageway that go nowhere in the less developed states of the union. It also shows two promising roads that were blocked through government intervention. But it would be wrong to cast central government as the perpetual villain and road-wrecker. In two major areas it has played an important part in supporting roads to genuine educational improvement. My direct involvement in these areas was limited and is somewhat dated. Nevertheless, from the trustworthy evidence of others, I am confident that these are genuine ways forward.

Until now, I have deliberately avoided naming schools or providing sufficient information for them to be identified. However, it would be hopeless, unnecessary and unfair to try to anonymise Thomas Telford City Technology College, now more commonly referred to as Thomas Telford School, or TTS. It is almost universally held in the highest regard. It comes near the top of the dreaded league tables; it is praised as excellent and outstanding by Ofsted inspectors. It is greatly over-subscribed by would-be parents. Yet it displays these traditional badges of success while managing to offer a curriculum and approaches to learning and assessment that are anything but traditional and share many of the characteristics of the 'joint enterprise' approach which have been previewed in the vignettes and initiatives described in the previous chapter.

Central government in general, and Kenneth Baker (the then education secretary) in particular, must take some of the credit for a remarkable achievement that has continued for 15 years. The original concept was a good one: setting up City Technology Colleges (CTCs) as 'beacons of excellence' making innovative and effective use of the new information technology and locating the colleges in or near areas of urban deprivation. The early history of the CTCs, which I know well, was chequered. As with any other group of schools, the CTCs were a mixture of good, average and poor – and one, TTS, that was from the outset, very good. I was privileged to receive regular evaluations from the inspectors whose responsibilities included regular visits to all the early CTCs. The inspector who visited Telford was even more of a perfectionist than inspectors were wont to be and hard to please. I was therefore surprised and delighted to receive a series of ever more positive evaluations of the school's quality. Such success can be partially ascribed to an exceptional founder head, and later to the long-serving and now knighted head who succeeded him. However, to have maintained a standard of excellence and continual development and expansion of its work over 15 years needs more than just outstanding leadership; the school judged correctly and applied consistently the essential strategies that lead to good education.

Much public information about TTS is widely available on the web and elsewhere, and its own website provides a wealth of quite detailed information, including the recent Ofsted report. This account is therefore selective. There are many features of what it does that are relevant to my theme. The Ofsted report refers to its "innovative and remarkably flexible curriculum". The school stresses the importance of capturing pupils' imagination, providing 'independent learning at all levels' undertaking interactive projects and promoting, self-reliance, confidence and teamwork. That these aims are not just wishful aspirations is clear from the sample curriculum extracts provided. These show that the learning is planned through both individual and group activities. They also show, in for example the Year 8 'totem' project, a valuable synthesising of more than one curriculum area. Billed as part of the art curriculum, it also covers history, philosophy/religious education and language. Though little detail is provided about assessment, TTS supports the concept of examination when ready, rather than at a fixed age. One consequence is that Key Stage 3 tests are taken a year early. It also attempts to tailor examinations to the needs and abilities of the pupil, rather than be content with the one-examination-for-all philosophy. Within the current rigidities of the public examination system this means entering pupils for a mix of GCSEs and GNVQs, (soon to be replaced by diplomas). While some criticise this policy as a way of improving the school's league table position, it seems improbable that this is the prime motivation in this instance. Another unusual but important feature is making what are normally extra-curricular activities an integral part of the curriculum. While lengthening the school day, it valuably blurs the line between 'work' and 'play' – more about this later in the chapter. The longer school day also allows longer sessions, matching the more broadly-based curriculum topics to longer periods of time focused on these topics, and doing away with the absurd 'all change after forty minutes' syndrome that has restricted learning in school for so long and wastes so much time in 'warming up' the brain, as well as the body in PE lessons. Breaks occur during the long sessions so that the learning process can be re-energised.

An anecdote from another walk of life, acting, may serve here to reinforce the notion of spending as little time as possible on warming up. After a recent, and memorable, performance of all three parts of Shakespeare's *Henry VI* on the same day, the cast held a question-and-answer session with those members of the audience who stayed behind after the third part. Asked about the impact of having to act in three full-length plays for over nine hours in a 12-hour period, members of the cast replied that they preferred performing three in a day to the three parts on separate days because both they and the audience, even with a lunch and supper break, were already warmed up for the second two parts, giving the whole thing a greater drive, and sense of achievement by the end. This is not to suggest a nine-hour school day (!) but to emphasise the point that the amount of learning depends as much if not more on what happens, or does not happen, during the day and how it is divided up as it does on the overall length of the day.

Two important recent developments at TTS are the preparation of on-line materials for other schools to use and the 'adoption' of nearby local schools. These two examples of outreach are fundamental to the concept of being a 'beacon' that was part of the CTCs' original purpose.

All this, to change the metaphor, amounts to an ointment of extraordinary value, which is not to say that it does not contain one or two flies. These need to be considered, not as criticism for its own sake, nor to diminish the school's outstanding achievement, but because they are relevant to any national scheme that makes use of the TTS approach. The main criticism is that the school is elitist because it is selective in its admission policy. Both 'elite' and 'selective' are contentious words and it is better to describe what appears to be the case in more concrete terms. TTS claims that it ensures that its intake is balanced in terms of IQ. However, the Ofsted report states that pupils on entry have a high prior attainment. In other words these pupils, before entering the school, are 'over-performing'. It seems to follow, therefore, that the school is selecting well-motivated pupils across the ability range that it judges will gain the most from a Telford education. There are many who would regard this 'selection by attitude' as perfectly justifiable. It could be argued that it is not inconsistent with the concept of 'equal opportunity'. However, this is not the place to argue the educational morality of selection by attitude. It is the place to point out that, because it selects already well-motivated pupils, TTS cannot demonstrate that its approach to learning serves under-performers well. To that extent it is not fulfilling one of its original aims of raising the achievement of under-performing pupils in the Wolverhampton area. Unless and until a previous education secretary's policy of admissions by lottery applies at Telford, its ability to motivate the hard core remains unproven.[1]

The second criticism relates to the use of information and communication technology (ICT). Some of the things that TTS does, such as make its curriculum plans available on line, are much better done by the use of ICT than by other methods. Other uses, such as replacing physical assemblies with televised broadcasts direct to classrooms, are less obviously worthwhile. No blame whatsoever attaches to the school for introducing this and similar technological strategies, for it was part of its original brief to do so, to experiment and find out whether particular innovations make for better education or not. It is possible, for instance, that the time and disruption saved by not having to move to and from assembly outweighs the loss of corporateness, shared pride, shared concern and shared grief, that such occasions can afford. Without trying one cannot be sure. Thus trail blazing, and not just for applications of ICT, are necessary to test and demonstrate whether a particular path does indeed lead forward. Assuming proper communication between schools, it is not necessary in any national system for the generality of schools to have to re-discover for themselves that certain paths lead nowhere or that other paths can reach the same place more easily. Nevertheless, there will always be the need for trailblazers, even in a stable and effective educational system. ICT is not the only thing that evolves, even if its evolution at present is much faster than most other areas of learning. Schools must always have the opportunity, and indeed be encouraged, to innovate, to seek new and possibly better ways of doing old things or trying something entirely new. While there are dangers in untrammelled experimentation, as a few schools in the 1960s demonstrated, these can easily be minimised through a sensible system of proportionality

---

[1] I would, however, be very surprised if TTS did not succeed with poorly motivated pupils to a considerably greater extent than do most other schools.

and accountability. Not too many risky innovations at any one time, trials and pilots before full implementation and appropriately timed external evaluation; not pulling up the plants before the roots have set – a frequent mistake by past governments – but equally, not allowing a noxious weed to spread.

Summing up TTS's achievement it is probably fair to say that it is about as good as it can be for the late 20th century but not good enough for the 21st. Once again, no blame attaches to the school for not having developed yet further. It is difficult to see how the school could have made more progress, given the restrictions imposed by the current English educational system, even if slightly relaxed for CTCs. It does not therefore serve as a complete map for an effective future system, but many of its features will be present.

An almost identical conclusion can be reached for the other enduring track though there are many differences of detail. This track is signposted 'nursery' or 'early years' education, and due credit must be given to central government for having instituted and supported this development. There is little doubt that nursery education – I prefer to use the phrase even though it is not strictly accurate – is a success. The proportion of nursery schools and classes, or settings to use the jargon, judged to be successful by Ofsted and other inspectors is high.[2] The historical reasons why nursery education is more successful than other phases are interesting but not directly relevant here, where it is more important to describe the features that make it successful. By now most of these will have a familiar ring. Most notable in nursery education is the removal of the line between work and play. This is not to suggest that all learning activities are 'fun' - play, too, can be purposefully stressful at

---

[2] A recent Ofsted report included some criticisms, particularly concerning the relatively weaker level of achievement by boys and in language development generally. The important point in this context is that Ofsted made no criticisms of the general philosophy and approaches to learning in the Early Years, but only of the sometimes weak application of these by certain schools and teachers.

times. The word suffers from ambiguity, as in the phrase 'play-time' to describe breaks in school learning; but there is an important difference between recreational activity and the kind of play that occurs within the nursery curriculum. The former takes many forms: messing about, lying around, 'hanging out', informal games and sports, and chatting over a cup of coffee, depending on age and preference. Recreation is deliberately a non-learning activity, though seemingly an essential one. Continual learning depends on it, for mind and body are incapable of continuous learning beyond a certain stretch of time.

The notion that play as an aid to learning applies only to nursery education is widely assumed, if not always openly acknowledged. Teachers of pupils entering a new phase of education are prone to assume that what was done at the previous school was not 'real' learning. As they grow older, pupils are pushed into an ever more passive and individual learning mode. Pressure of examinations becomes increasingly the justification for this, and from the age of 14 these are an almost constant presence. The reality is that play is a powerful tool for learning to the end of secondary education and beyond. Only in drama lessons, where it is integral to the subject, is regular use made of it, yet it can add zest and depth to learning at any age and subject. Good teachers have long known this and made effective use of it. Play is not necessarily any less intellectually challenging than 'real work'. Two, very different, anecdotes illustrate this. The first is taken from one of the best history departments it was my privilege to experience, where sixth-formers were asked to play a kind of card game to 'get inside' the heads of those involved in the religious debates that raged in England during the 1650s. This slice of history is a challenging and potentially rather tedious one for heavily secularised late 20th century sixth-formers. A lecture by the teacher, that many might have justified 'because this topic is too difficult for you to tackle on your own through the textbooks' might well have engendered more boredom than learning. However, in the context of the game, the sixth formers became heavily involved in the theological and social arguments; with timely and judicious intervention by the teacher their learning was both rapid and deep. The second example will outrage some readers as it is drawn from England's most radical school, Summerhill. Perhaps its best-known feature is that pupils may elect not to attend lessons, and during what the school terms 'the gangster years', roughly age 11 to 14, many choose not to do so. During an inspection, one inspector spent some time observing what the 'gangsters' actually did during the lessons they missed. The results were interesting. A group of pupils took themselves off to the large sandpit in the school grounds where they proceeded to excavate and build an elaborate network of tunnels and 'fortifications'. The high quality of the discussion and decision making that went on within the group, and the understanding that grew about the nature of materials and forces meant, in the view of the inspector, that the time spent on this activity was a valuable learning experience, possibly more so than the lesson that they would otherwise have attended. This is not to suggest the Summerhill approach should be part of a national system – though the slightly less radical idea of offering some choice of learning activities is worth considering. What is significant is that, even without teachers' planning and supervision, pupils are capable of learning through play.

In 2000, appropriately for the new millennium, the government defined the Foundation Stage curriculum as 'everything that children do, see, hear or feel in their setting, both planned and unplanned. Replace 'setting' with 'school' and 'children' with 'pupils/students' and the definition is equally applicable across the whole school age-range. This definition leads on to further consideration of the nature of the nursery curriculum and it proves to be the second reason for the success of nursery education. The curriculum has many strengths. The first is that it is all embracing. There is no dividing line between National Curriculum subjects, religious or personal and social education. A single set of areas of experience in the Foundation Stage covers the whole range of learning. As a result, the educational experiences that need to be provided can be considered as a whole and can draw in as many of the areas as makes sense. This avoids the artificial subject barriers that particularly affect the secondary curriculum. These barriers create two problems. The first is organisational. Separate planning by different heads of subject leads to unplanned repetition, omissions or different messages imparted by different subjects. These problems are soluble in theory but in practice require a degree of communication between subject departments that is rarely achieved because of other pressures on the teachers concerned.

A more serious problem is the compartmentalisation of knowledge in the minds of pupils. Pupils from the age of five increasingly experience education as a series of mental rooms where they spend a short while picking up a little learning before moving on to another room, probably unconnected. Not surprisingly, pupils store their learning in separate compartments and seldom make any links between the learning in each. This even occurs, on occasion, within subjects as well as between them, as the following amusing but telling anecdote demonstrates. In the course of inspecting a primary school and observing a mathematics lesson, I started talking to a nine-year-old pupil with the somewhat inane but harmless comment – "I see that you are doing some maths this morning". I received a withering look and a testy reply, as though to say "what is this idiot on about?" – "This isn't maths it's SMP [school mathematics project]; we do maths on Wednesdays." "Ah, I said", recovering from this onslaught, "tell me what you are doing in SMP then." Clearly maths and SMP were two entirely different subjects in the mind of this girl. No wonder that the chief weakness in pupils' mathematical learning is their inability to apply skills that they have acquired even to new mathematical investigations, let alone to problems in other subject areas that require the use of numbers.

A second consequence of the all-embracing curriculum is the lack of division between extra-curricular and 'intra-curricular' activities. Activity of any kind during the school day contributes to learning. The lowering of the artificial barrier, as it exists for the later age-groups, between what is compulsory and essential and what is an optional bonus, assists pupils in making links between areas of knowledge and applying skills learnt in one area to another.

The last noteworthy feature of nursery education is its enlightened and effective approach to assessment and recording. In strong contrast to what happens later on, the government wisely restricts its requirements to a broad set of Early Learning Goals, to be reached by the end of Foundation Stage, while offering guidance to teachers on how to facilitate children's progress towards these by means of Stepping Stones. The actual assessment is left to the teachers themselves, with some degree of validation through periodic external inspection. The final recording is in profile form – Records of Achievement properly reborn for a different age group as the Foundation Stage Profile. The various elements of the goals for each area are a judicious mixture of knowledge, understanding, skills, attitudes and actions, both individual and joint, and are concerned with continuing development as well as specific achievement. The language goal, for instance includes:

- 'enjoy listening to and using spoken and written language' (attitude);
- 'explore and experiment with sounds...' (individual action);
- 'interact with others, negotiating plans...' (joint action);
- 'extend their vocabulary' (development);
- 'speak clearly and audibly' (skill);
- 'know that print carries meaning' (knowledge);
- 'show an understanding of the elements of stories' (understanding).

No external examinations are needed. Assessment is undertaken by the teachers as an integral part of the teaching and learning process. Schools are free to devise their own detailed systems of assessment provided that they are compatible with the overall assessment and recording framework. In the most recent development, the rather too crude measure of either achieving or not achieving a particular goal has been superseded by a nine-point scale, linked closely to the curricular Stepping Stones as well as the Goals themselves. This finer grain assessment makes it a suitable approach for any age group and has the potential to provide nearly all the information about a pupils' individual and group achievements and attitudes that gatekeepers to employment and further education need or can reasonably expect. The small remainder, based on the Record of Achievement model, involves pupils' self-assessment and self-recording of their perceived achievements.[3]

In one additional way nursery education points the way forward. In devising the curriculum, its assessment and recording, the government and its agencies have worked closely with a range of educationalists, from independent consultants through to schools known for their good practice. (Again this is reminiscent of the ROA model.)

All in all, nursery education is a good deal more than just an enduring track; it is the start of a broad highway, capable of leading on to ways of learning suitable for the 21st century and, with modification of detail to suit older pupils, the basis of a national system across the compulsory years of education, and perhaps beyond. It will be a tragedy if government, weighed down perhaps by hidebound attitudes, potential costs, top-down pressures, bureaucracy or sheer inertia fails to capitalise on the success of early years education and apply it across the age-range. The very recent further evolution of the Department of Education and Skills into the Department for Children is good in principle in that it encourages an all-embracing approach to children's development that includes their welfare and personal development as well as the more academic side of their education. However, there is a danger that the ever-increasing bureaucracy of 'child protection', however well intentioned, and its understandable focus on 'safeguarding' may divert time and energy away from 'promoting' children's welfare.

---

[3] In my ignorance I originally supposed that pupils of nursery age were too young for meaningful self-assessment. I was glad to be proved wrong by the reference in the 2007 Ofsted report to outstanding practice in assessment: "In the best examples, children received regular feedback and were encouraged to make their own assessments."

Achieving the right balance between reducing risk and encouraging initiative is difficult. The temptation for government, after every well-publicised child tragedy, to tighten further the risk net with short-term measures threatens to undermine this balance.

Chapter 4

Fellow Travellers

Ivan Illich – Martin Chilcott

It would be the height of arrogance to pretend that the ideas put forward in the preceding chapter are the unique products of my brain. Many others have seen the merits of, written about, and in some instances are starting to turn into action, the various approaches to learning that have been described and recommended. In this sense they are fellow travellers of mine along the same or the same kinds of roads and tracks. This short chapter acknowledges this fact and demonstrates that clear-sighted ideas about learning can come from a variety of sources, and not the most obvious ones. The two examples I have included come from near the start and the end of the forty-year period, from very different personalities, ideologies and walks of life. Given that the sample is tiny, the fact that there is such convergence of ideas about good education proves nothing, but it at least suggests that seeing the right way forward in education is not dependent on a particular view of the world or set of assumptions.

The first fellow traveller fits the secondary meaning of the phrase, 'ideological political adherent' rather well. It is none other than Ivan Illich, remembered by educationalists, if at all, as the 'notorious de-schooler' and, I confess, thought of by me in the 70s and 80s as a danger to education, much quoted by those extreme educational militants within the ILEA who tried to destabilise its schools, and sometimes came close to doing so. But a recent article by Charles Leadbetter in *Prospect* magazine has opened my eyes to the value of some of his ideas.

Leadbetter describes how Illich saw that the main achievement of what he called welfare capitalism was to create large-scale public service institutions concerned with such key matters as health and education. While the intentions of welfare capitalism were benevolent, designed to deliver services that were fair and reliable, the systems required to implement these intentions tended to dehumanise the process. The institutions involved in implementing the system not only provided the services that people needed; they defined their needs. In some ways, therefore, the welfare institutions actually exacerbated the problems they were set up to solve. Because formal schooling involves telling pupils exactly what they need to learn, some pupils' learning is inhibited rather than enhanced. Furthermore, formal school creates the impression that learning is something that only occurs within the confines of a single place, the school, at a particular stage of life, and with the help of a single group of people, the teachers. Young people are not, therefore, encouraged to see their learning as a process that continues throughout their life nor to seek learning from a wide range of sources beyond school. The way that the school education system operates encourages pupils in the belief that the process of education is mainly concerned with certification rather than increasing personal self-development; that it is complete and comes to an end when the final certification has been achieved.

Illich's analysis of the problem is persuasive; some of his solutions Leadbetter rightly describes as dotty, but others 'do chime in with many aspects of the internet age.' These include what is now referred to as 'lifelong education', providing access to learning resources at any time in many places other than schools; libraries, offices, museums and so on. Another idea is to make it easy to provide all those who want to share knowledge to connect with those who want to learn through skills exchanges. What sounded far-fetched in 1971 Leadbetter now describes as 'the conventional wisdom of social networks'. He acknowledges that professionals, i.e. teachers in the context of school education, would remain the most knowledgeable players in any given field but would find themselves operating alongside other sources of knowledge and refers to the potential of such things as the internet and computer games that involve player developers. Some of this seems like heady stuff to the older generation of educationalists such as myself but for those growing up during the information revolution it is part of the natural way of doing things. The important point in this context is that schools should not regard themselves as educational islands or monopolistic suppliers of learning. As the information age develops, the practical difficulties of involving a wider range of human expertise and learning resources in the process of school education diminish. What TTS has done in this area is just a start.

A second fellow traveller, Martin Chilcott, Chief Executive Officer of the Place Group, is putting time, money and business expertise where his mouth is. As a successful businessman, he is poles apart from Ivan Illich but his basic beliefs about the realities of schooling are remarkably similar. His starting point, providing buildings that are fit for 21st century schooling, is different but equally legitimate and rooted in a perceptive understanding of the essentials of the learning process. Though I find his vision to be overly concerned with the utilitarian dimension of education as opposed to its life-enhancing role, this is no more than a matter of emphasis and part of legitimate debate that has raged since Plato and Aristotle about education for the good life versus education for the good citizen. His educational foundations are sound. Suitable buildings are not an absolutely necessary condition for effective schooling, but they are desirable requirements for fully effective learning. Most existing school buildings constrain rather than facilitate effective learning, not necessarily because they were poorly designed in the first place but because even the better designs lack the flexibility that enables them to adapt to changing educational needs. The government has now recognised the need for a major rebuilding programme for 21st century schools. One can only hope that it and its partners will not be seduced by any current and short-lived educational fads and fashions into adopting inflexible building designs that repeat the mistakes of the past. If they heed the ideas put forward by the likes of Martin Chilcott, the buildings now under construction will be more likely to accommodate future developments in school education than those built in England during the previous two centuries.

Chapter 5

Salient Features, Redundant Features

Salient features for the future in curriculum, organisation, assessment and reporting, school buildings, resources; archiving for academic and vocational, broad and balanced, mixed ability et al, national standards and examination system.

Old maps show post houses and tollgates. Today's road atlases and sat navs show petrol stations and speed cameras. (Tomorrow's maps may be back to tollbooths again!) As with road maps so with the map of education. This chapter summarises the salient features that would characterise an era of joint enterprise. It clears away unnecessary and unhelpful words and concepts that bar the way forward and have led to some costly diversions.

Everything up to this point has been secondary to the main purpose of this book, which is to set out how pupils and children should be educated until they leave school. It has been historical, anecdotal, occasionally autobiographical and deliberately loosely structured, with the intention of providing a narrative context and explaining the need and the rationale for the new educational Atlas.

The second part of this book lacks narrative, mainly because the story has yet to happen! Whereas this first part has intentionally rambled across the decades and different facets of education, the second part is much more structured. Its chapters are tightly focused on a particular aspect of education. Readers may, therefore, find the second part heavier going than the first. To mitigate this problem, in part at least, I have included some examples to compensate for the missing anecdotes but only sparingly, for what I hope are two good reasons. The first is that stuffing the text with examples tends to obscure the logic of the arguments. The second reason is it is difficult to produce convincing examples of something that does not yet exist; especially so when these would need to be drawn from subject disciplines and areas of learning in which I have little or no expertise. Specialists might rightly be critical of the details in the examples and this could lead them, wrongly, to criticise the general principles of the proposals. I have, therefore, limited my use of examples to those sections of part 2 where an over-reliance on abstractions and generalisation might otherwise threaten comprehension. If readers are stimulated to come up with better examples than those I have made up, well and good.

This final section of part 1 should be seen, to use a musical metaphor, as a bridge passage between the two parts. It draws from the preceding narrative what will become the salient features in the new educational map but without attempting to locate them precisely or consider their implications for educational provision. It is because these implications are considerable that we require a new atlas containing several maps, not just a single, new map. Consequently, the aims of part 2 are both to restate the essentials of effective education and explain how they can be achieved. This involves a re-working, not only of how schools function, but also of the shape and organisation of the whole school educational system.

But before setting off down the new road in earnest, it is opportune to pause and reflect on the lessons learnt from the many failures and isolated successes of the last forty years. What are the salient features in the new Atlas? What can join the tollgates and post houses in the archives?

Nearly all the points listed below have been exemplified in previous chapters, some repeatedly. A few, particularly concerning assessment and management, have been implied rather than explicitly mentioned.

The two chambers of the heart of any educational system are the ***curriculum and approaches to learning***. Their salient features in the new map will be:

- an all-embracing curriculum, as already exists for nursery education;
- a holistically devised curriculum drawing on curricular and subject areas as and when they are appropriate;
- a greater proportion of time devoted to pupils undertaking joint working;
- stronger emphasis on pupils learning actively, making decisions, taking responsibility and meeting deadlines;
- less emphasis on knowledge devoid of context and on the imparting of knowledge by teachers;
- integration of extra-curricular activities with the curriculum;
- a greater element of choice at all ages;
- accreditation of 'trailblazer' schools to pilot possible new curricular approaches.

To facilitate effective learning in response to the curriculum, changes will be needed in curricular and school ***organisation***:

- a longer school day for most;
- mainly longer lessons/sessions;
- grouping of pupils as appropriate to the nature of the enterprise, not necessarily by age;
- no homework for most.

A major change of practice will be needed to ***assessment and reporting (A&R)***. This will include:

- most A&R undertaken by teachers, not external bodies;
- most assessment done during lesson time through observation and questioning;

- a reduction in the marking of written work;
- schools devising their own assessment systems within a national framework;
- increased pupil self-assessment and self-reporting;
- Records of Achievement, along the lines of the ROA project and the Foundation Stage Profile.

As funds become available, ***school buildings*** will need to change to:
- reflect curricular and organisational changes;
- provide the flexibility needed to accommodate curricular and organisational evolution.

The range and use of human and physical ***resources*** will need to be regularly reviewed and updated to make best use of advances in information and communication technology and sources of support and expertise beyond the school staff.

Changes will be needed in ***governance and management*** to manage the changes needed and to involve representatives of parents and all other elements of the local and regional communities in consultation, decision making, personal and financial contribution and feedback on:
- the curriculum;
- the learning process;
- the recording process;
- resources and buildings.

A new network needs to be established for ***communication, school and curriculum development, support, validation and accountability***, particularly in relation to:
- curricular development and validation;
- co-operation between schools;
- sharing of resources, resource development and information exchange;

- monitoring and advising on school performance;
- training of teachers and other practitioners.

Various words and concepts can be consigned to the educational archives. Getting rid of the phoney distinction between 'academic' and 'vocational' education is perhaps the most important. There have never been widely agreed definitions of either. All learning is to a degree academic and to some extent vocational. Arguing about the nature and merits of the two is a sterile debate which has undermined the effectiveness of both the curriculum and the examination system and should be abandoned.

Abandoned also should be the concept of a 'broad and balanced' curriculum. Both breadth and balance are relative terms incapable of precise definition. In reality, most school curricula below the sixth form lack breadth because they give no attention to economics, law, philosophy, psychology or sociology. Newer curricular areas such as media studies and travel and tourism, which have direct relevance to the lives of nearly all pupils, are usually provided only for a minority in an intellectually unchallenging form and pilloried as 'soft options'. Furthermore, a curriculum made up solely of a series of subjects, however numerous, lacks breadth if taught in an unrelated way because it misses the important elements that link or overlap subjects. Nursery education realises the need to bring together various kinds of 'knowledge and understanding of the world'. Higher education has long ago recognised the value of such cross-over subjects as astro-physics and socio-biology.

So-called balance is defined in practice by existing norms. A visiting Martian or a 14th century cleric would find hard to understand that balance means eight periods of mathematics and one of religious studies. Determining balance, as normally happens, by the frequency of lessons in each week is a rigid and unhelpful way of facilitating learning. The concept of balance needs to be replaced with that of 'due proportion'. A proportionate curriculum recognises that the acquisition of some essential or desirable skills is intellectually challenging and takes more time than the acquisition of other skills or knowledge. For most of us, the calculus is harder and takes longer to learn than map co-ordinates. It acknowledges that some understanding grows slowly and to a degree unpredictably dependent on mental maturity while other comes as a sudden 'road to Damascus' realisation. It also recognises that different skills require different units of time to be effectively learnt, and different contexts. It is easier, for instance, to learn French, or Mandarin, or Arabic, in a community that speaks these languages than through three lessons per week in an English-speaking school. Determining due proportionality is hard but essential. A start to tackling this will be made in part 2.

It is worth retaining only half of the often bracketed concepts of 'continuity' and 'progression' replacing 'continuity' with 'consistency'. Achieving 'continuity' in education is normally thought of as ensuring that no gaps are left in the order in which a subject is studied. However, even in the present system and in the supposedly most linear of subjects such as mathematics, it is difficult to agree on what constitutes a 'gap', and history syllabuses are unavoidably full of gaps. In a system where subjects are not the main determinant of curricular development, the concept of continuity becomes even more difficult to sustain. But consistency is important in any system. The same topics need to be taught in the same way using the same terms and methods regardless of where they occur in the curriculum if pupils are not to become confused. Of course, as children mature, the methods become more sophisticated and the terms more numerous and technical but previously used terms need to be retained as the starting point.

'Progression' is sometimes regarded as mere education jargon, used in preference to 'progress' in order to make the speaker or writer appear more professional. This is mistaken. 'Progress' is what children make; 'progression' is a feature of curricular planning undertaken by practitioners. Well-planned progression makes it easier for pupils to make progress; conversely, poorly planned progression inhibits progress. It is for, example, a commonplace that many pupils currently fail to make progress during their first year in secondary school. While there are other factors that may be involved, the main reason for this lack of progress lies in the weaknesses of schools' planned progression. Normally, this is because secondary school teachers are unaware or dismissive of what primary school pupils can and have achieved so that there is no 'stepping-up' in conceptual challenge. Occasionally, planned progression fails because the step up is too large or because intervening steps are omitted. Getting consistency and progression right at the planning stage is not easy; nor is the process of checking these. This issue will be taken up in a later chapter.

It would be difficult in practice to erase the word 'ability' from the language of education, but all those cognate phrases, mixed ability, lower ability etc., that imply that ability is a single measure need to be outlawed. We need the help of psychologists perhaps to come up with a set of reasonably simple words that best describe the varying profiles of potential for learning and performing that pupils present. Until that time, we should always link the concept of ability as a noun or adjective to a particular skill or discipline, an able musician, weak in numeracy, reading age around average. When we have to define the characteristics of a particular group it needs to be done in terms of specific areas of potential or performance, high-performing track athletes, mixed capacity for mental mathematics, well-developed entrepreneurial skills, varied natural drawing abilities, and so on. If this makes for clumsy prose so be it; it is a necessary price to pay for avoiding the inaccurate and unhelpful labelling of pupils that decreases their chances of learning effectively; and which also leads, for some pupils, to depressed self-image and low confidence and, for others, unwarranted arrogance based on the notion that intellectual prowess is the only yardstick. This is purely an argument about words and concepts. The issue of how best to group pupils for learning is something entirely different and will be tackled in part two.

It would also be good to consign to the archives all those words that describe how well or badly pupils do, achievement, attainment, performance, standards; particularly the last because of its shift of meaning from what should be achieved to what is achieved. Different educational bodies make up their own definitions of these words, which then conflict with those of others, causing considerable confusion and wasting time that could be used more profitably. Words that describe changes in how well pupils do, such as progress and value added, suffer equally from conflicting or inaccurate definitions. But it is a pipe dream to hope that they can be dispensed with wholly. As with ability, we need to avoid generalised statements about achievement, progress and the like and express all statements about what pupils can do in as concrete and precise a form as possible. Also, the scope of how well pupils do needs to be enlarged to encompass achievement, or whatever we call it, in the all-embracing curriculum as defined for the Foundation Stage.

To advocate the banning of loose, over-generalised statements about achievement does not imply any denial of the importance of periodic monitoring of what pupils can do on a school, regional or national scale. We all need some reliable way of checking how well the system is working, but a more efficient and less costly way of doing this has to be found than the present expensive, time-consuming and crude measurement of 'national standards' through a bloated universal and repetitive examination system. Part 2 considers some possible ways forward to achieve this.

No doubt there are plenty of other words ready to be confined to the 'recycle bin', including much unnecessary educational jargon that obscures rather than illuminates the process and results of learning. However, dwelling on current blemishes, though easy, is of limited use; we need to move from failures of the past and present to the challenges of the future.

Part 2: The Future

Chapter 6

Prelude: What's in a Name?

Searching for a new term – joint enterprise – joient – the decline of metaphor – the future present

The English language, rich though it is in synonyms, has been so heavily used by educationalists that it is difficult to find an existing word to describe something new which does not come with a history or overtones that send out the wrong messages. In searching for a single word that would convey the essence of what, until now, I have termed 'joint enterprise' I tried and rejected many words. 'Topic' has negative overtones as applied to the wishy-washy primary school curriculum of earlier decades. Topics all too often forced together wholly disparate subjects that shared only a weak semantic link. 'Project' is a good but frequently used word, but it implies a one-off special undertaking rather than a continuing system, which is what this work aims to describe. 'Undertaking' has some merits but has overtones of coercion. Similarly, 'task' implies something prescribed and quite possibly unpleasant. 'Activity' has some merits because it emphasises that learning should not be passive but it already has a common use in education as something that happens outside the classroom and the formal curriculum. 'Exercise' is too redolent of boring and repetitive 'sums'. 'Venture' is tempting, with its overtones of adventure and setting off with a purpose into the unknown. However, 'enterprise' is still better, sharing some of the characteristics of 'venture' but with the added entrepreneurial element; more rooted in everyday reality, and less exceptional like Operation Raleigh expeditions. Also, 'enterprise' is only marginally used by educationalists, notably in the phrase 'Young Enterprise'. But on its own, 'enterprise' sounds too individual. 'Joint enterprise' diminishes the egoistical element and signals the importance of working together: pupils with pupils, teachers with teachers, schools with schools, and all of these with each other and with other providers of knowledge, understanding, skills, support and finance. However, 'joint enterprise' is a bit of a mouthful and not the stuff of which memorable sound bites are made, seemingly a necessity in our modern, high-speed, age. So I decided to invent a word that would compress the two-word phrase into one. The word is *'Joient'*. In addition to containing the whole of 'joint' and part of 'enterprise', it has overtones of enjoyment, to which all education should aspire if not always achieve. The 'ent' suffix also suggests a developing process, as for example in 'crescent moon' or a continuing, active state such as 'incandescent', rather than something inert. Whether the word ever catches the public imagination and enters the language is unpredictable. It is not particularly mellifluous, but then neither is 'chav'. At all events I shall use *joient* in preference to 'joint enterprise' throughout part 2. I am less concerned, however, with the survival of the word than with what it describes. The rest of this part will attempt to ensure that the proposals at least enter the public consciousness, whether or not they ever become practical reality. I am all too aware that, as in the parable, many good seeds fall on stony ground and that many of those that do take root in the public consciousness do not come to full fruition, for all kinds of unpredictable reasons, usually wholly unconnected with the merits of the organism. Darwin does not rule in human affairs; the fittest do not always survive. However, inaction means certain failure; one can but cast the seed and hope.

So 'joint enterprise' disappears from the text from now on. The Atlas and associated cartographic metaphors continue, but in attenuated form. The reference to blind alleys, paths, tracks and highways served as a heuristic device in part 1; but all running metaphors eventually reach the end of their usefulness and become constraining rather than illuminating. The chapters that follow are still presented as pages in the new Atlas but, where metaphors are used, they make more varied comparisons. Most of the language used, however, is direct, for dressing up new ideas in metaphorical clothes is usually a way of disguising their lack of clarity.

I also decided to use as the prevailing tense in part 2, the future present: that is writing about the newly described world of the joient curriculum using the present tense as though it is already in existence. Stylistically this seemed preferable to the constant use of the future simple, 'will', or future conditional, 'would'. The fiction that the newly described world actually exists should not, however, be taken to indicate whether or not it will ever come into existence. I deal with the likelihood of that happening in the final chapter.

I have adopted the word 'practitioner' as used for Early Years education for general use across the whole school age-range in preference to the much more familiar word 'teacher'. This is not intended in any way to imply a reduction in the status or importance of qualified teachers in assisting pupils' learning. It does, however, signal that teachers are but one of a group of people who are involved in helping pupils to learn. Teachers are the 'general practitioners' of the education profession and, like medical GPs, do the bulk of the work. But they are far from being alone. As in the medical profession the likes of practice nurses and paramedics continue to increase in importance, educational practitioners of all kinds will play an increasing role in the learning process.

Chapter 7

The Joient Curriculum

The varied nature of the joient curriculum – ACKS – cross-curricular joients – due proportion – Areas of Learning, modified for older pupils – fundamental and desirable elements – school discretion in planning joients

The most important characteristic of the joient curriculum is that it cannot be precisely defined. As with the Foundation Stage curriculum, its detail varies from school to school. However, all schools have some curricular elements in common and work within a nationally prescribed curricular framework.

The second most important characteristic of the joient curriculum is that it consists of a series of joients not subjects. The constituent elements of every joient are attitudes and actions, concepts, knowledge and skills (ACKS). The addition of attitudes and actions to the traditional trilogy of knowledge, concepts and skills is crucially important as it bears directly one of the fundamental purposes of joient, to improve pupil motivation by getting them involved in doing things. It is not as radical as it might at first appear for it already exists in the Foundation Stage curriculum, as described in chapter 3. Attitudes and actions are two sides of the same coin and therefore count as a single 'A'. A pupil may have a particular attitude to learning but very often this can only be recognised as existing through a related action. To return to the earlier example of the

Foundation Stage goals, the fact that a pupil 'enjoys using spoken language' is made apparent by the action of 'exploring and experimenting with sounds'.

The third characteristic is that all joients involve ACKS from more than one and usually several curriculum areas. The number of curriculum areas involved and the emphasis given to any one of them varies. This variation will be considered in the next chapter.

An attribute of the joient curriculum is that, collectively, the joients cover the all-embracing curriculum in due proportion. The national curricular framework specifies the required elements, in terms of ACKS, and the due proportions. Deciding what these proportions are is a challenge because it is a new idea but it is made a little easier in that the proportions devoted to particular elements are stated in terms of range rather than precise percentages of the whole curriculum or the numbers of hours per week. As argued earlier, the concept of curricular balance is a flawed and subjective one. Schools have the right and the obligation to decide upon the precise proportions of the various elements provided they stay within the prescribed ranges.

This leads on to the question of what these elements are. If they are not to be set out as sub-sets of subjects, how are they to be described? The first answer is that it does not really matter what labels are given to replace subjects and how the various elements are grouped under them. However, the phrase that is most neutral in its implications and has the merit of already being in use is that adopted for the Foundation Stage, namely 'Areas of Learning'. While there are various other valid starting points for labelling, the Areas of Learning used to describe the Foundation Stage curriculum are as good as any other for the rest of the school age-range. However, the definition of the areas requires some modification or elaboration to reflect the growing range and complexity of the learning that is required.

In the area of personal and social development, for example, some of the general goals suitable for early learning require little or no modification. Being confident to try new activities and initiate ideas remains as important at age 15 as it is as at age 5. Similarly, sensitivity to the needs and views of others remains a key attitude and action, but, to match pupils' increasing maturity, by age 15 the definition of 'others' includes people not immediately present or personally known. Other social and personal goals such as 'dress and undress independently' require substantial re-interpretation, while retaining the base concept, in this example the significance of dress and the messages it sends out about the individual or the group. It hardly needs stating that teenagers are acutely conscious about clothes and body image. The point that needs emphasising is that the curricular proportions given to dress and other less obviously intellectual areas remain broadly the same throughout the school curriculum. The over-emphasis on subject knowledge that characterises the present secondary curriculum is avoided.

This work is an atlas not a complete set of 1:25,000 Ordnance Survey maps. It does not therefore begin to attempt a detailed transformation of the whole Foundation curriculum to the primary and secondary phases. It draws attention only to one or two major features. One significant difference between the present Foundation version and the joient area of communication, language and literacy, is that the latter includes information and communication technology, with the emphasis, naturally, on the uses of information and communication rather than on the technology. It also includes consideration of other modes of communication, Braille and sign language for example, and in some instances acquisition of skills in such areas. This is not just a 'special needs' issue. Mainstream schools may have good reason to foster the development of alternative communication skills. Also included within the category of 'other modes of communication' are the much maligned media studies. Awareness of how people make use of, abuse and manipulate a combination of written text, speech, sound and visual images to convey an ideology, market a product or create a disposition for action is a crucial piece of learning. It is not, of course, a 'subject' nor even necessarily referred to by name but its curricular content has a potential place in many joients, for example, one on propaganda, including its role in Nazi Germany or Mao's China, or the creation of an advertisement for selling a consumer product, drawing on current TV advertisements.[1]

At first sight it might appear that as pupils grow older the greatest changes and modifications are needed in the area of 'knowledge and understanding of the world'. After all, as even primary teachers might argue, this includes the whole of science as well as the humanities subjects, not to mention the social sciences that the existing school curriculum largely ignores. But to split this area up into sub-areas of, say, science, humanities and social sciences and plan for each of these separately would be to undermine the whole joient philosophy. Take for example the Foundation Stage elements of looking for similarities, patterns and change, why things happen and how they work. These issues are central, not only to all the sciences, but also to geography and history, technology, sociology, psychology, politics, economics and even philosophy, the last of these now finally being recognised as something from which all pupils can potentially learn. I wrote disparagingly in an earlier chapter about the 'one-invention-after-another' approach to the First Industrial Revolution. However, a joient focusing on the transformation of England from an agricultural to an urban society can provide the context for a great deal of scientific, technological, geographical, and sociological, as well as historical learning.

To cut short what is in reality a long story, the development stage of the joient curriculum requires that the Foundation Stage

---

[1] I still vividly remember a superb media studies lesson in which a class was led by the skilful teacher over a 40-minute period to deconstruct a 30-second Audi advertisement. As we watched the whole clip for the final time at the end of the lesson, we all were aware of how very differently we all saw it and felt about it compared with our first viewing. Our learning was considerable and the skills we had acquired were readily transferable to other advertisements or presentations.

curriculum elements are reviewed in detail, adopted and modified as necessary while maintaining approximately the same level of generality for the curriculum framework. How this should be done and by whom is also the subject of a later chapter. What is attempted here is an outline of what sets of elements are likely to figure in the framework.

All the elements have already been defined as attitudes and actions, concepts, knowledge or skills (ACKS). An important sub-set of all these elements is those that are fundamental. Fundamental elements are similar to but broader than the present concept of 'basic skills'. They include the skills and understanding in literacy and numeracy that are essential pre-requisites of learning in other curricular areas, but they also include the fundamental concepts or skills needed for learning in other subject areas. Examples of such fundamental elements are the basics of literacy involving sentence structure, punctuation and the use of capitals to impart meaning; an understanding of place value in numeracy; of weight and mass in science; the concept of space as represented by maps and globes in geography, time as represented by dating systems in history and the relationship between supply and demand in economics.

A difficulty soon arises in deciding what is fundamental, what is desirable and what is unnecessary. Subject proponents always argue vociferously for the inclusion of much more learning in their area than is actually necessary for most pupils. This includes a good deal of mathematics and English language as well as those other subjects already inside the school curriculum and others struggling to gain entry into it. It is asserted that certain topics are essential for the further study of the subject at A level or university level. Such assertions are spurious. University departments of ancient and modern languages have learnt to live with the fact that their students may arrive with no subject knowledge or subject-specific skills and yet reach degree standard, and many other university courses start from the position where their students know nothing.[2] The idea that a great corpus of knowledge built up over several years is a necessary pre-requisite for effective learning in a particular subject discipline at a higher level is demonstrably false and a form of 'educational feudalism': special pleading by subject leaders to preserve, or preferably to enlarge, their curriculum baronies.

If subject specialists are given free rein, as with the previous National Curriculum subject working parties, the result is a bloated and disproportionate conglomerate curriculum. Here it is only necessary to emphasise the necessity of not repeating this mistake. A later chapter suggests how it might be avoided. But to exclude desirable elements from the required framework of fundamentals does not necessarily exclude them altogether from the joient curriculum. Once again, the Foundation Curriculum guidance offers a way forward with its 'Stepping Stones' and 'Examples of What Children Can do'. Such indicative guidance assists schools in developing its own programme of joients; it can also act as a checklist for evaluating draft programmes before finalisation and guard against unintended or unjustified gaps. The expectation is that all schools will cover a majority, though probably not a large majority, of the desirable elements.

But it has to be recognised that even with an extended school day, the scope of the all-embracing curriculum means that some of what is currently included in subject syllabuses and which specialists would regard as desirable, cannot be included amongst the elements. Where a particular school feels strongly that it wishes to include a subject topic not mentioned in the curricular framework, it can still do so provided that it can make out a good case. The mechanism by which schools gain agreement to their proposed curriculum is considered in a later chapter.

---

[2] The army showed how this could succeed half a century ago when it taught sufficient Russian to some of its National Servicemen in a matter months, if not weeks, to become effective members of the Intelligence Corps.

In part 1, the idea was put forward that pupils' learning is enhanced by giving them a chance to make some choices about what, and how, they learn. However, in the joient system this choice is realised differently from the present secondary system of 'options'. The joient curriculum is the same for all the pupils in a particular school up to the end of compulsory education. The present difficulties about what subjects to drop or to choose no longer exist and there is no danger of wrong choices affecting later career ambitions. However, pupils have opportunities in most joients to make choices, both individually and in groups, about how they tackle the work and, within the broad topic of the joient, what specific parts of it to study.

This chapter, or page of the Atlas, has given a 'satellite's view' rather than a bird's view of the joient curriculum. The next pages of the Atlas provide larger-scale maps of the territory, in particular, the nature of individual joients and how they are devised. To summarise what this satellite's view shows, the joient curriculum is marked by the following:

- a national framework of compulsory fundamental elements defined in terms of attitudes/actions, concepts, knowledge and skills;
- division into Areas of Learning based on those used in the Foundation Stage, with weightings for these stated in terms of duly proportionate ranges;
- national guidelines setting out the desirable elements across all areas of learning;
- individualised school curricula, incorporating all the fundamental elements, a majority of the desirable elements and any other agreed topics within the duly proportionate ranges allowed;
- curricular organisation by joients, not subjects, that involve more than one curricular area;
- a common curriculum for all pupils in each school but with pupil choice built into most joients.

Chapter 8

Planning Individual Joients

Joient length – planning joients – learning and pupil directed aims – preliminary remedial learning – pupil actions – time limits – assessment

This page of the Atlas outlines the general nature of individual joeints by considering factors that affect their length and by going through the planning process. Exactly who is involved in the planning process is the subject of a later page in the Atlas.

An important point to note is that joients are of no particular length. They can be planned to last no more than a few minutes or they can stretch over at least half a term. Both these extremes are exceptional. Most joients last for between the equivalent of one full school day and two full school weeks. The longer ones are not continuous so they will take anything from several days to several weeks to complete, longer still where real-time events are involved, such as growing plants.

The length is determined primarily by the aims of the joient and its consequent nature. Those that aim to make a simple, though not necessarily obvious, point that requires only short-term pupil action and little 'finding out' can be completed within an hour. An example, if it were a one-off, is one of the individual mixed-age projects in the girls' independent primary school described in chapter 3. Those joients that require extensive research using ICT or other sources of evidence need much longer, as do major undertakings that contain several stages and interim aims, as for example one that involves identifying a need, designing and making a product, costing and marketing it. Most joients, however, fall somewhere between these extremes.

The length of a joient is also influenced by its planners' judgement of the 'learning stamina' of the pupils who take part. Other things being equal, shorter joients are more appropriate for younger and more extended ones for older pupils. But other things will often not be equal. The high degree of motivation involved in joients with a strong intrinsic attraction for a particular group of pupils enables them to persist for longer than might normally be expected. Such joients are likely to include those that have a considerable 'reward' at their end, such as devising and participating in a play or other performance, finding 'treasure' or seeking to win a competition. The range of abilities amongst pupils involved may also be a factor but the caveats expressed earlier about the multi-faceted nature of ability have to be borne in mind.

It is difficult to make generalisations about the content of any single joient, because the potential combination of elements from the various areas of learning is virtually limitless. Most joients cover curricular elements from several areas of learning, but a few, where a new fundamental element is being introduced, are more restricted in their curricular range. Where a new fundamental element is involved, the greater part a joient may be concerned with acquiring this so that sufficient time is provided for pupils to learn something quite new to them. But it is never the case that a whole joient is devoted to a single fundamental element. There is no such thing, for example, as a mathematics lesson entirely divorced from the rest of the curriculum. Even these almost single-element joients have to include pupil actions designed to enable the newly learnt element to be practised and placed in a real-life, proxy or play context.

The proportion of joients within the whole programme devoted primarily to the acquisition of fundamental elements is variable. For younger pupils, who have many fundamentals to acquire, the proportion tends to be higher than average. As pupils grow older the emphasis shifts from fundamental towards desirable elements and towards reinforcement and greater synthesising of existing attitudes/actions, concepts, knowledge and skills (ACKS), rather than the acquisition of new ones.

Planning a joient is a complex process. It can be simply described as moving logically from a consideration of the learning-directed aims to be achieved, to choice of a topic area, to fashioning the pupil-directed aim, to deciding the details of the process, the resources needed, the modes of learning to be adopted and the assessments employed. The reality is rather more complex. Various constraints of time, resources, practitioner expertise, second thoughts following unexpected changes in circumstances and the need to fit the various joients into a coherent, all-embracing whole require a process that involves a good deal of modification, back-tracking, compromise and fine-tuning. At times the process is reminiscent of the frustrations in trying to complete a Rubik cube or similar puzzle, but it also gives rise to the satisfaction of succeeding. To aid understanding of what joients are like, however, what follows mostly ignores the complications and proceeds through the stages in turn.

The first things that have to be considered are the learning-directed aims: what learning area elements is this joient intended to address? Most likely it will include some of the ACKS from several areas. The particular combination agreed leads to a consideration of possible topics that would be a suitable vehicle for fostering the learning of the chosen elements. (In practice, it is possible that some 'good' topics are put forward first and these are then considered for what elements could be included.) One example might involve elements drawn from the subjects of biology and history to develop pupils' understanding of cause and effect in both these areas with particular reference to epidemics. Various possibilities immediately present themselves: cholera, influenza, plague, AIDS and so on, with the first of these chosen for the example that follows.

Once the general area of a topic is agreed, the next step is to find an approach that will 'hook' pupils. This becomes the pupil-directed aim that clearly states an end product or end result to be achieved within a set deadline and a mode of achieving this that requires pupil action. For example "the aim is for each group to make a 20-minute presentation to a non-specialist audience to explain what cholera is, how it became a scourge in 19th century London, how its causes were isolated, how the disease was eventually eradicated from London and what measures need to be taken today to eradicate cholera worldwide."[1] Whatever the aims and the combination of areas of learning involved, all the aims relate to the world in which pupils operate, in real-life, simulated real-life or play situations. In the example given, the aim is simulated real-life. Pupils make the presentation but in groups to each other or another class. What real-life is and what kind of play depends on the pupils' situations. Though there is increasingly a common youth culture, regional factors, urban/rural differences and changes in what is topical and fashionable may affect the precise way in which the aim is formulated.

The third stage is to consider what ACKS pupils need before they can make a start on the joient, to assess the extent to which they possess them and, if necessary, plan for 'remedial' learning to take place, either for the whole group or for those individuals that, for whatever reason, have not yet acquired them.[2] In the cholera example, pupils need some prior general knowledge of bacilli and

---

[1] Of course, it does not have to be London, though that is the city for which the historical evidence is probably the most accessible. But it could equally be Manchester, Glasgow, or indeed Calcutta if that what the school decides and is able and willing to make sufficient evidence available.
[2] I am not using 'remedial' here in a sense that implies past failure by pupils or slow learning. Though these may sometimes be the reasons why pupils have not learnt the necessary elements, the cause of the gap in learning is unimportant. The important thing is that it is filled.

understanding of how they interact with the human body. In a perfectly constructed programme of joients, all pupils have had the opportunity to acquire the necessary elements. In reality this is impossible to achieve in every case, hence the need for some remedial teaching. Though it might appear logical, where the need can be assessed in advance, for this to take place before the main part of the joient begins, it may well be better to allow pupils to realise for themselves the elements that they lack and then respond with pre-planned remedial teaching.

The fourth stage involves planning the range of things that pupils will do and deciding the acceptable limits and time constraints for these. One aspect of the concept of due proportion is ensuring that pupils have sufficient choice and freedom of action within realistic limits. The planned degree of constraint on time and range of action tends to diminish as pupils grow older. This helps to foster the element of pupils taking increasing responsibility for their actions and for organising their time. In the cholera example, the main area for choice lies in decisions about what methods and materials to use in making the presentation, how to share out the work between the group and how to divide the time available between research, preparation of materials and 'rehearsal'. Pupils' choice of information sources, textbooks, internet, teacher input etc. is unfettered in principle but in practice constrained by what is available.

The fifth stage is concerned with the provision and use of resources to maximise pupils' opportunities for learning. Provision of resources includes deciding on and making available the practitioners who will be involved; also the availability of other sources of information, accommodation and facilities within or beyond the school. Use of resources requires decisions to be made on how and for how long practitioners introduce the joient and give guidance, on how much, if any, direct teaching and individual remedial support is required; also on strategies for intervention as the joient proceeds, or shows signs of not going according to plan. Such decisions are highly dependent on the nature of the joient and the characteristics of the particular groups of pupils involved. They involve the kind of teaching skills that are already highly developed amongst effective practitioners.

In the light of all the planning up to this point, the penultimate planning stage involves a decision about how long the joient needs for completion. Once decided, the deadline is added to the pupil-directed aim. (Again, in reality, planning may run up against time constraints earlier in the process and these may affect the aims and nature of the joient.) The cholera example probably merits about twelve hours in all, spread over about three weeks, but might have to do with less because of other time pressures.

The last stage is concerned with finalising the assessment arrangements; finalising rather than deciding from scratch because assessment implications are usually implicit within the approaches to learning already decided. Nevertheless, it is rare for all the potential assessment opportunities to be realisable in practice. Decisions are needed about priorities as to what is assessed. A later page of the Atlas considers assessment in more detail. It suffices here to emphasise that assessment is an integral and essential feature of every joient, is mainly done 'on the hoof' rather than as a mountain of marking at the end of a joient or the end of the year, and provides the vast majority of the information that leads to the overall assessment and recording of pupils' performance. Some joients, and particularly those near the beginning of a school year or phase, are deliberately designed more for their assessment than their learning potential. They seek to establish or confirm the capacity and potential of pupils in a particular group in respect of selected ACKS with a view to using the results to fine-tune future joient planning. In these instances, assessment-directed aims take priority over learning-directed aims although they do not replace them entirely; stand-alone assessment instruments are not part of the joient philosophy.

Time to summarise the main features. Individual joients have the following characteristics.

- They are variable in length to match the aims and contents of the topic and the nature of the pupils.
- They all include learning-directed aims and pupil-directed aims.
- A minority include assessment-directed aims and all contain some assessment procedures.
- A minority make provision for learning a particular fundamental element; these cover a narrower than average range of elements drawn from other areas of learning.
- All include plans to achieve due proportion in allowing pupils choice and freedom of action.
- All include planned provision of human and other resources for information and guidance.
- All include plans for pupils to use these resources to maximise their learning, for practitioners to be available to provide direct teaching, individual support and appropriate intervention as and when needed.

Chapter 9

Curricular Development

Sources of support for schools, central, regional, advisers, other schools – principles for joient programmes – planning matrix – regional accreditation – medium and short-term planning

The previous chapter touched on the fact that the development of a programme is complex. It is also a long and challenging process, especially when tackled for the first time. Whilst the final decisions about the details of the programme are taken by individual schools, subject only to external accreditation; this does not mean that every school has to develop its own programme from scratch. Though all schools have particular features and situations that their programme needs to reflect, they also share many characteristics. There is no reason why they should not use the same joients with only minor variations. It would be a wasteful duplication of effort and excessively time-consuming for every school to develop a separate programme in isolation and without assistance. This chapter describes, in broad terms, how various groups of people support schools in developing the programmes and how the schools themselves need to tackle the planning process. Later chapters consider in greater detail the formation, composition and remit of these support groups and how the organisation of the school can facilitate the planning of joients.

A minor complication lies in the differences between curricular development during the initial stage of introducing the joient system and when in its steady state. During the introductory period schools need to rely more heavily on external support; in the steady state this diminishes unless the school itself is changing significantly.

Schools have four sources of support. The first of these is at national level. A body, similar to the existing Qualifications and Curriculum Authority (QCA), initially devises a sizeable sample of model joients across the curricular and age range.

For planning purposes these joients are labelled in terms of both the areas of learning most strongly involved and the age-range of the pupils for which they are intended. Between 5 and 16, age-ranges are defined as lower and upper primary, and lower and upper secondary[1]. These models also include samples of short, average length and longer joients to exemplify the range of time-span as well as the variety of content.

The models have two purposes, the first being to provide a starting point for school curricular planning. Schools are not required to use them either in their precise form or at all, but are strongly advised to study them carefully and adopt or adapt them appropriately. The other purpose of the models is to provide starting points for the development of joients by the second source of support, the regional bodies.

These bodies have multiple responsibilities which will be described in a later chapter. In the context of curricular development, their task is to develop a complete set of joient programmes to cover the whole curricular and age range and take account of the geographical, historical and socio-economic characteristics of the region. As with the nationally provided models,

---

[1] As explained in the introduction, the main parts of the Atlas are concerned only with schooling up to the statutory leaving age. However, the principles of the joient system apply equally to the sixth form. What should perhaps happen from age 16 is briefly explored in part 4.

schools are not required to adopt them. Their choice ranges between wholesale adoption, through selecting a proportion of joients from each programme, to developing their own programme unaided. In the introductory phase schools are likely to opt for something closer to wholesale adoption with only minor adaptations and gradually move towards a greater proportion of school-initiated joients.

The third source of support is the provision of advisers. Whereas the national and regional support is essentially static and one-way, the advisers provide support that is dynamic and interactive. Their function in the context of curriculum development is to work with schools in the development process, to offer expert advice where sought but not to determine the programme or the content of individual joients. The amount of time an adviser devotes to a particular school depends both on the extent of school's own capacity to develop its programmes and the degree to which it adopts joients from the regional programmes.

The fourth source of support is other schools. In the long run this is likely to prove the most efficient and effective means of support. Given the advances in ICT, it is easy for schools to share their curricular plans, as already demonstrated by Telford. Regional bodies have the responsibility of setting up a joient bank into which schools are encouraged to 'deposit' their joints, and which they can draw on in order to supplement their own planning. Additionally, especially in the introductory stage, local groups of schools can agree to share out the process of developing joients by learning area and/or age-range.

Notwithstanding all these sources of support, each school still has to put its own programme together and finalise the details of each joient. The following principles have to be borne in mind:

- All learning areas relevant to the nature of the joient need to be included.
- A majority of desirable elements and all of the fundamental elements have to be covered within the programme as a whole.

- The programme must maintain due proportion.
- There must be consistency and progression within and between programmes for successive age ranges.

To achieve the first three of these requires an age-group-related team of practitioners drawn from all the relevant subject specialists. These are most likely to be sub-phase teams, for example, class teachers and subject specialist teachers of pupils aged 8-11. This method of curricular planning is widely practised already in nursery and primary schools for whom it does not, therefore, pose great difficulties. Planning across learning areas is much more challenging for secondary schools, accustomed to devising their curricula as conglomerations of subject syllabuses.

The key tool in both phases is the 'planning matrix', plotting the various elements to be covered in each joient and using the matrix to ensure that in the programme as a whole these are present in due proportion. A typical matrix is a simple computer spreadsheet program that schools can use 'off the shelf' or develop for themselves along the following lines. The row headings of the matrix give the name of each joient, the column headings are concerned with the aims, time and duration planned, the elements within each area of learning and the assessment scales to be used. Once provisionally agreed by the planning team, the details are completed for each joient in turn. As the details of each joient are entered, the total time devoted to each area of learning and its constituent elements are calculated so that planning team are reminded of the need to achieve due proportion and enabled to make any necessary adjustments.

Precisely how the school organises and times its planning process is its own decision but each team has to prepare annually its draft matrix for consideration by the school's senior management, heads of house and heads of school, whose responsibility it is to check that the curriculum is sufficiently all-embracing and duly proportionate, but also, crucially, to check for any discontinuities or lack of progression.[2] Regular interchange of matrices between the planning teams within schools to ensure consistency and progression during the planning process should mean that the time needed for final checking by senior management is not too great and allows for some fine-tuning. Nevertheless, it remains a demanding task. Senior management checking is not just a paper exercise, though that is the first step. It also requires discussion with the planning teams so that managers can probe those areas of the planning where consistency and progression are unclear.

Checking by senior management is not, however, quite the final stage of the planning process. One consequence of the move from a National Curriculum to a national curricular framework is that schools have to be accountable for what they decide. The sometimes disastrous curricular free-for-all of the 1960s must not be repeated. For that reason, schools have to submit their planning matrices to the regional body for accreditation. In the introductory stage this will be particularly important but it is not a heavy handed or dictatorial process. This accreditation is analogous to a MOT, a certificate of curricular roadworthiness, not an in-depth critique. In the great majority of cases, schools 'pass' first time. A few require minor adjustments and resubmission of the joients that need modification in order to achieve accreditation. A very few, that is those where the curriculum is seriously flawed, fail accreditation completely. These few schools, in the first instance, receive intensive support from an adviser and, as a last resort, are required to follow a curriculum devised for them. In the early years after introduction, schools need to have their curricula accredited annually. Over time, as schools regularly demonstrate their ability to construct a curriculum that meets the basic principles, they are only required to apply for accreditation every three years, unless they plan major changes.

---

[2] The management structure needed for schools is set out in the next chapter.

The total time planned for in the matrix needs to be between 80% and 90% of the total curriculum time available. Sufficient time is needed to allow for various contingencies: joients that turn out to require longer than expected, unforeseeable national, regional, local or school events and incidents that pupils need to come to terms with or that curtail the learning time available. A small amount of time is also needed for 'bright ideas' that crop up unpredictably and which cannot be accommodated within any of the planned joients.

By definition these additions or adjustments to the programme can only be planned at short notice so the planning teams need to meet regularly throughout the school year, not just during the main planning process. Such meetings are also required to put flesh on the bones of the matrix. Some of the detailed planning of individual joients, as described in the previous chapter, may need to be undertaken well in advance. For example, teams need to ensure that appropriate resources are available, such as booking accommodation at outdoor centres or arranging for artists in residence. However, the planning for most of the detail of how the joients are to be implemented is best undertaken in the medium-term, termly or half-termly. The fine detail, reacting to what practitioners learn about the nature of the pupil groups and their abilities, requires weekly, even daily planning. Nursery and primary schools are accustomed to these methods of planning. For secondary schools this requires considerable changes of practice. It is clear that the planning teams need to be in a position to meet easily and frequently. How schools might organise themselves in order to achieve this is the topic of the next chapter.

Chapter 10

Organising the school

Over-large secondary schools – deployment of staff – school units and planning teams – contact with 'partners' – implementing the joient programmes – responsibilities and remuneration – grouping of pupils – deployment of time – the 'third session' – extension tasks – specialist learning – optional studies – community action – tutorial sessions – resolving clashes

The present structure and organisation of both primary and secondary schools make them less than fully fit for the purpose of operating the joient system but primary schools are much more nearly fit. This mismatch is hardly surprising given that both primary and secondary schools were set up to operate an earlier system. Primary schools used to be under-staffed, allowing practitioners too little time to plan the curriculum and monitor it, but the increase in the number of classroom assistants in recent years has gone some way to redressing this problem. In secondary schools one of the main problems that affects both the present system and the joient system is that most schools are too large to make practicable the kind of flexible approach that the joient system requires. The bloated size is a consequence of attempting to create viable sixth forms in comprehensive schools, an attempt which largely failed. The prohibitive cost of physically reducing the size of schools and building additional schools with smaller numbers rules out these measures as practical proposals except in the very long term.

Fortunately there is a way of minimising the diseconomies of large schools without building new ones, in effect creating two or more 'mini-schools' within the buildings of an existing large one, operating autonomously in all routine matters.[1]

For the purposes of this chapter 'organisation' is taken to include the deployment of staff, the grouping of pupils and the use of time. These are considered in turn.

Most present-day secondary schools operate using a 'mesh structure', combining the horizontal 'weft' of year-groups, mainly for pastoral purposes, with the vertical 'warp' of subject departments, mainly for academic purposes. Many add a second vertical strand, in the shape of 'houses', mainly for competition in sporting and other activities. However, the conflicting tensions between the vertical pull of subject demands and the horizontal pull of pastoral concerns does not, as in a mesh, create a strong seamless robe but rather threatens to divide pupils into separate pastoral and academic beings. Most schools are aware of this dichotomy and do their best to ensure effective liaison between teachers with, respectively, pastoral and subject-based responsibilities for particular groups of pupils. However successful these arrangements are, their cost is high in terms of the time devoted to the systems of communication. The larger the school, the more time-consuming the liaison arrangements and the greater the likelihood that they fail to function effectively.

The organisation of primary schools tends to be simpler and more effective. Both pastoral and academic responsibilities are combined in the class teacher. The difficulty that class teachers face of having sufficiently wide-ranging subject skills is met by grouping class teachers together in year-group, sub-phases or Key Stage teams. This comes close to what is needed in the joient system for both primary and secondary schools.

---

[1] This is said to be generally working well In New York city - see *Herszenhorn, David. "In New York's Smaller Schools, 'Good Year and a Tough Year'." New York Times 8/08/05* – and has recently been proposed for England by 'Teach First'.

In the joient-friendly model described in the following paragraphs the suggested numbers are indicative only and are based broadly on current staffing levels of one practitioner per 16 pupils. Local conditions will necessitate some variation in the numbers. In both primary and secondary schools the practitioners include both fully qualified teachers and support staff, such as nursery nurses, workshop technicians and laboratory assistants.

The basic school unit numbers 320 pupils and 20 staff. This is divided vertically into two houses of 10 staff and 160 pupils and further sub-divided into two teams of five staff and 80 pupils each normally spanning three year-groups. (The upper secondary years, given the continuation of the current statutory school leaving age, contains only two year-groups, except for any fast-learning pupils who join the upper secondary phase ahead of the normal age-range.) In what follows, a team of five is referred to as the planning team. In reality its role is much wider than just planning and encompasses all aspects of educational provision 'at the chalk face'.[2]

Unlike existing practice in many primary and almost all secondary schools, curricular responsibilities start from the 'bottom', that is to say with the planning teams. The initial planning of the joient programme is the joint responsibility of each team. At the start of the planning process, the house planning teams responsible for the same sub-phase need to collaborate. How precisely the planning work is divided is a matter for the teams to agree. For example, each house team could plan half a term's work, or practitioners from the house teams with particular interest in or expertise one of the areas of learning could plan the joients where this area predominates.

The planning teams do not do their work in isolation from the outside world. Although theirs is the responsibility for completing the programme, as much as is feasible they need from an early stage

---

[2] The number five refers to the full-time equivalence of the team. For various reasons connected with practitioner training and educational government, dealt with later, most teams will probably consist of more than five people.

to involve 'partners' who are not education professionals in the planning process. Early involvement is important because partners need to feel and to be integral to the curricular development process, not critics of an almost finished draft. Partners include parents, governors, people from the local community and any other 'friends of the school'. Such involvement undoubtedly creates practical difficulties but these need to be overcome because of the great benefits that the partners bring, not only through their different areas of experience and expertise but because of the commitment to the successful implementation of the plans that their involvement encourages. For younger pupils, this is especially true of parental involvement as the Ofsted 2007 report on the Foundation Stage clearly demonstrates. As pupils enter the difficult years of teenage puberty, when they tend to rebel against their parents' attitudes and lifestyle, the involvement of well-known or influential local figures can offer them positive alternative role-models to boost and maintain their motivation.

Once the process of finalising the planning matrix is complete, as described in an earlier chapter, each house planning team is separately responsible for putting the flesh on the bones in the medium-term planning stage, and also for the short-term, fine-detail planning. This does not rule out further co-operation between parallel house teams if this is how they wish to plan but, with some exceptions, this is not necessary. The exceptions concern the use of scarce resources and accommodation. As far as possible the school is divided into house zones and each house operates largely within its own zone and with its own resources. Where this is not possible, for example because there is only one gymnasium or one specialist music teacher per school, then there needs to be prior agreement as to how the use of scarce resources is to be timetabled. These exceptions apart, houses are free to differ in how they develop the planning matrix and implement it. They also plan their use of the 10-20% contingency time independently, except when some unexpected incident or event that affects the whole school necessitates a common response.

As described in the previous chapter, the curricular role of heads of house, together with the head of school, is primarily that of checking for consistency and progression and ensuring that the other basic principles of matrix planning have been adhered to before submitting it for accreditation by the regional body.

Individual heads of house also have a responsibility for checking the medium-term planning undertaken by their planning teams and for monitoring both the fine-detail planning and actual implementation of the joient programme with a particular eye for consistency and progression. The monitoring involves the same range of strategies already used by effective schools: direct monitoring of lessons; discussion with pupils while joients are in progress about their learning, and when they are completed about their achievement; attendance at planning team meetings and scrutiny of assessment arrangements and their implementation.

Responsibilities for assessment and pastoral matters also start with the planning teams. How assessment is undertaken is the subject of a later chapter. The way in which pastoral matters are handled closely matches current primary school practice. Though the planning group members are jointly responsible for pastoral care, it is likely that each member of the team will act as tutor for a group of up to 16 pupils so that every pupil has a first point of contact. Nevertheless, pupils are encouraged to relate to all members of the planning team, indeed to all the house staff. The head of house is only involved with individuals in particularly difficult cases.

Team planning by staff, hardly a new idea, remains a fundamental part of the joint enterprise system. Planning from the bottom upwards is currently less common but is no less fundamental to the joient philosophy of giving the maximum amount of control in the planning process to those who will be implementing the plans.

The school management structure in the joient system is simple and 'flat'. This work does not venture into the treacherous quicksands of teacher pay and remuneration. Suffice it to say that because most responsibilities are jointly held, and that because the number of senior managers is kept as small as possible, practitioners' remuneration is not based on status within the elaborate hierarchies that currently exist, especially in secondary schools. All practitioners are deemed to have some special areas of expertise, whether in particular subjects or other education aspects, so this expertise in itself is not a reason for additional pay. However, where practitioners demonstrate particularly high levels of expertise, they accrue additional roles beyond the school as a later chapter explains. These roles attract additional pay so that the concept of rewarding high quality performance remains.

The grouping of pupils differs considerably from current practice. Planning groups are responsible for the learning of 80 pupils spanning the year-groups. The default mode of organisation can be considered as three separate year-group classes of 26-27, with one practitioner in charge of each, leaving at least two 'spare'. However, for all kinds of reasons to do with pupils' capabilities, practitioners' expertise and the nature of the joients, the number and composition of the groups differ; ranging, where accommodation allows, from an introductory lesson for a single class of 80, through various combinations of mixed-aptitude and mixed-age groupings, where the team judges that these combinations best suit the pupils and the nature of the task.

The likelihood is that all members of the team are actively involved for much of the time in helping pupils to learn or assessing their progress and achievement. All have a proportion of 'non-contact time' though, unlike the present rigid school timetable arrangements, the amounts may well vary from week to week. There are occasions, especially in secondary schools, where subject specialists from another team need to be 'borrowed' for a particular session. Despite this, the implication is that the planning teams will be responsible for ensuring pupils' learning in all of the joients for most of the time across the whole range of the curriculum. This is not a daunting prospect for primary practitioners but does pose a considerable challenge for those in secondary schools. The re-training implications are considered in part 3.

The deployment of time is radically different from the current system that operates in most schools though it bears a strong resemblance to the Telford approach. A key feature of the joient system is the extension of the school working day and a corresponding reduction in out-of-school work for both pupils and staff.

The school day divides into three sessions. Two of these sessions last for approximately 2½ hours, including short breaks amounting to no more than 30 minutes, for all ages of pupils. The third session varies in length broadly in proportion to pupils' ages; shortest for the lower primary stage and longest for the upper secondary.

The first two sessions are devoted to implementing the joient programme and any contingency plans. The third session is for everything else other than a relatively short mid-day break[3]. It contains a mix of components. One of these, at least so long as the law continues to require it, is the daily assembly and act of worship. Most assemblies are by houses and held simultaneously where the accommodation allows it.

A second component of the third session consists of 'extension tasks', undertaken by groups or individuals. These are usually, but not invariably, related to particular joients, and have clear and manageable short-term aims. They replace homework and include, amongst a wider range of possibilities, the current homework tasks of reinforcing learning acquired during a joient and acquiring knowledge, for example of Spanish vocabulary, needed for a joient's next session.

A third component is 'specialist' learning, individually or in groups. This is provided for pupils who need specific additional help

---

[3] Organisationally it would often be possible to do away entirely with a standard lunch break and this occasionally happens in English schools and commonly elsewhere, for example French Lycees. However, pupils tend to resent being unable to meet up with friends whose lunch breaks are differently timed and the social and pastoral loss is probably greater than the organisational gain.

or specialist learning. The 'additional help' is to solve a particular learning problem identified during a joient and needing immediate attention. It is likely to be a one-off occasion, or at most very short-term provision of remedial learning. Specialist learning is something that lies outside the elements of the curricular framework but is required by a particular group as part of a joient. It is usually something that cannot easily or efficiently be acquired by pupils in the course of their normal learning. An example is the skill of using a specialist piece of technical machinery that pupils would not in general need to have.

A fourth component consists of optional studies. These include particular aspects of traditional subjects but also a much broader range of learning, such as sporting, intellectual and creative activities. These are superficially similar to the choice offered in present-day extra-curricular activities programmes but are determined not by the school but by the enthusiasms of individual or small groups of pupils. They are largely pupil-initiated and pupil-run apart from any adult supervision needed for health and safety reasons or expert support. In principle, the range of opportunities is infinite, but limited by practical considerations.

A fifth component is community action. This phrase encompasses a wide range, including community work of various kinds but also such things as work experience, local activism, such as lobbying for a children's playground to be re-furbished, and undertaking social surveys. Practitioners are responsible for facilitating the community action programme and the necessary supervision but, wherever practicable, respond to proposed actions suggested by the pupils.

A sixth component consists of tutorial sessions carried out by assigned tutors with individuals or small groups of pupils. These form an integral part of schools' assessment and recording policy and are built round the 'Pupil Profile' system to be considered in the next chapter. Schools and houses have discretion in the details of the way they organise the tutorial system. A typical allocation of time in a secondary school is half-an-hour per pupil once a fortnight, requiring each practitioner to devote up to four pupil-hours per week to tutorial work. Holding tutorials with pairs of pupils, therefore, consumes up to two hours per week of practitioners' time in the third session.

Third-session timings are kept as flexible as possible. A few, such as assemblies, are fixed in advance. Where the demand is known in advance, adult-led activities, such as specialist learning, community action and sports fixtures are timetabled. Other pupil-adult meetings, such as additional help, are negotiated between the pupils who want or need them and the practitioner concerned. Tutorials have an outline timetable but this can be amended by negotiation. Extension tasks and optional studies are timetabled by the pupils themselves in the third-session time slots available.

All this makes for a complicated and sometimes difficult programme to achieve. On occasion there will be 'clashes'. An individual pupil wants to attend two components that take place at the same time. Practitioners find themselves in danger of being double booked. This complexity is not to be regarded as a structural weakness but as something that contributes to the overall learning process. Pupils, and staff, have to decide priorities and sometimes negotiate alternative arrangements and timings to avoid clashes. Learning how to do this, and how to live with compromise solutions, are amongst the life skills and attitudes that pupils need to acquire.

Chapter 11

Assessment and Recording

Current A&R weaknesses – joient A&R strengths – ensuring comparability – A&R segments – ongoing assessment – terminal assessment – group assessment – self and peer assessment – assessment by partners and parents – third session assessment – external testing – Record of Achievement

It is an unavoidable fact that assessment comes under the heading of 'important but boring'. General readers may, therefore, prefer to skip the technical detail that takes up most of this long chapter and merely take note of the differences between the present-day and the joient systems of assessing and recording pupils' achievements set out in the bullet points below. Assessment and recording (A&R) are vital and integral parts of the joient system, and the methods used are radically different from the prevailing external system of testing and examination.

Current national A&R systems suffer from multiple weaknesses:

- lack of clear and useful links between internal school assessment and external tests and examinations (except for limited links in the national tests and predicted examination grades);
- excessive emphasis on an external examination system that is expensive, bureaucratic, time-consuming, flawed in its

effectiveness and efficiency and too narrowly focused on one aspect of achievement;

- reliance on 'moment-in-time' assessment, either at a specified age, or as has recently become fashionable again, 'testing when ready';
- lack of any formal recognition of pupil self-assessment;
- over-elaborate systems for monitoring national standards;
- ineffective in indicating progress made by individuals and schools over time.

Joient A&R is the antithesis of all of these:

- most A&R carried out by practitioners as an integral part of the joient programme;
- minimal emphasis on external national tests and examinations; reduced bureaucracy and expense;
- all areas of learning assessed in due proportion;
- primarily ongoing A&R, ensuring that any 'rogue' results are identified and discounted;
- account taken of pupils assessing themselves and each other;
- a sampling method for monitoring national standards;
- measurement of progress integral to the A&R process.

The present national system purports to ensure comparability of standards through national external bodies – though it adopts the strange strategy of using several, commercially competing, examination boards to do this. The joient system is no less concerned with ensuring national comparability and fairness but does so in a radically different way. It places the main onus for assessment on practitioners but ensures that they work to a common set of rules. The main instruments for assessment and recording are the Pupil Profile, having strong resemblances to the present Foundation Stage Profile in the use of scale points related to learning goals, and a revived version of the former Record of Achievement project for acknowledging more broadly defined aspects of achievement.

The assessment objectives for every joient are directly related to the learning-directed aims, which in turn are based on the elements of the national curricular framework. These objectives re-define the curricular elements – the learning goals of the Foundation Stage – in terms of matching assessment scales. Sometimes the phrasing of the scales is little more than the rephrasing of an aim or aspiration in terms of an achievement. One of the Foundation Stage goals for writing, for example, includes the phrase 'begins to form simple sentences, sometimes using punctuation'. The matching statement for point 9 of the Foundation Stage Profile, which is defined as going just beyond the goal, is 'communicates meaning through phrases and simple sentences with some consistency in using punctuation'. Often, the assessment scale provides more precise detail of what constitutes achievement than is evident from the goal. For example, one of the social development goals is stated as 'forms good relationships with adults and peers'. Point 9 of the assessment scale sets out what form this might take: 'Takes account of the ideas of others'.[1]

I have deliberately chosen to quote point 9, the top end of the Foundation Stage scale as it might reasonably become point 1, the bottom end of the equivalent lower secondary scale. Excluding pupils with severe learning difficulties, a six- or seven-year gap in 'learning age' is fairly typical between the lowest and highest achieving pupil. For the lower and upper primary phases, as described in chapter 9, there would be varying degrees of overlap between the scales used for successive phases.

---

[1] The full sets of scales for the Foundation Stage are set out in the DfES publication *Foundation Stage Profile Handbook,* 2003 and available on-line. The handbook provides detailed examples of how the achievement of a particular scale point might be achieved. The national curriculum and assessment framework for joients needs to contain similar material for the guidance of practitioners and others concerned to measure pupils' achievement and progress.

The following example may help to clarify how the link between goals, or learning-directed aims, and assessment scales works out in the joient system. A typical joient for a lower secondary group, around 12 years old, might consist of devising and producing a ten-page booklet designed for next year's new pupils, describing the school, what to expect, what to do, who is who etc. The booklet has to be completed to a tight deadline and has to contain photographs. The gist of this forms the pupil-directed aims. Because the set of assessment scales are centrally determined for each area of learning, the assessment criteria for this joient – and for all others – have to be related to and consistent with the national scales, but the decision about which of these to use and how they need to be customised to fit the nature of the joient from part of the team's planning. The practitioners decide that the learning directed aims should be drawn from three areas of learning together with their related assessment scales. These are:

- <u>Personal social and emotional development (PSED), focusing on team operation under pressure and meeting deadlines</u>. The assessment criteria reflect such things as the degree of each individual's success in contributing to the team operation and meeting the deadline. They take into account such features as allocating time for different sub-tasks, including devising text, taking photos, collating the material and 'publishing' it; also the degree of commitment and focus on the essential tasks, and success in coping emotionally and practically if things go wrong or get behind schedule.

- <u>Knowledge and Understanding of the World (KUW)</u>, focusing on the ICT skills of taking technically competent photographs and successfully importing them into the booklet, and the creative skills of composing the photographs and placing them in the booklet for maximum effect. The ICT assessment scale considers speed as well as technical competence. The creative scale considers 'media studies' issues such as effectiveness in linking the pictures to the text and captions as well as the artistic merits of the photographs themselves: composition, use of colour, contrast etc.

- <u>Communication, Language and Literacy (CLL)</u>; focusing on the production of factually accurate, informative, relevant text written in a language register suitable for the potential readership; also on the choice of apposite captions for the photographs.

Some mathematical skills are also required for the successful completion of the task, particularly those concerning place, shape and measures, in working out the combination of words and size of pictures needed to fill the ten pages. On this occasion the practitioners decide not to assess the mathematical skills formally, so as not to overload the assessment process. There is always a potential for over-assessment and a temptation to squeeze the maximum possible assessment out of every topic. Assessment 'experts', that is to say those who design but do not carry out the assessments, are the most likely to succumb to this temptation. Practitioners, however, quickly learn from their experience of attempting to scale 'marking mountains' about what is possible and practicable so it is right and proper that they should be mainly responsible for deciding how and what to assess. However, it would be possible in this example for the relevant mathematical assessment scales to be included in the initial planning of this joient and one of the other areas of learning excluded. This change might have to be taken in the light of review and monitoring by senior managers if they judged that assessment in the joient programme as a whole was too light on the mathematical area of learning. The decision about this would, therefore, be taken in relation to the other joient assessment arrangements within the planning matrix, reflecting the need to ensure that all assessment scales are sufficiently but not excessively covered. A change in assessment arrangements is more likely if this joient is one of those planned early in the curricular development process.

Assessing in relation to a common set of assessment scales and scale points, centrally defined, goes a long way to ensuring comparability between schools, but to ensure that practitioners have an agreed understanding of what the scale-point definitions mean in practice, visiting moderators make sample visits. These check that practitioners are not under- or over-assessing pupils' achievement and progress in two ways: first, that pupils' level of achievement is being assessed and recorded at the correct level; second, that practitioners are undertaking enough, but not excessive assessment. Just as with curricular development, the prime responsibility for assessment lies with the planning teams working to centrally prescribed parameters and subject to monitoring both within and beyond the school.

The A&R system contains several segments. These differ in size for reasons that are explained below. The great majority relate to the assessment of individual pupils but one is concerned with group assessment, and one with overall national levels of achievement.

The largest segment is that of ongoing assessment during the course of a joient. This is undertaken jointly by those practitioners involved in implementing it. Normally, this is by members of the planning team. Exactly how the team goes about gathering evidence for assessing the point on the assessment scale that pupils have reached is for its members to decide. In the example given above, for instance, the team might decide that four practitioners, each reflecting their particular area of subject expertise, concentrated on a different area of learning: one on PSED, one on CLL, with two working together on the ICT and creative elements within of KUW. Much of the evidence, as in this example, comes from direct observation or listening so as to judge whether pupils have mastered a particular skill, developed a particular attitude or acquired a piece of knowledge that they know how to apply. On occasion, particularly to check understanding, it is by focused questioning during a session. This questioning may be pre-planned, asking the pupils why they chose a particular feature of the school to photograph, or it may arise from pupils who claim to be 'stuck', for example not being able to size a photograph to the desired dimensions, providing evidence about what it is they do not understand or cannot do. The inclusion of unplanned questioning within the formal assessment process illustrates the point that teaching and assessment, though separate in principle, are often intertwined in practice.

Most ongoing assessment, however, is pre-planned and part of the joient planning. Because for much of the time joient practitioners working with the class are facilitating and supporting rather than directly teaching, they have opportunities to undertake systematic assessment. However, there are occasions when a practitioner is needed whose primary role is assessing rather than facilitating learning. This is an important part of the role of the 'spare' practitioners in the planning teams. They are not usually needed – indeed will not be available because of other commitments – for all the sessions devoted to the joient but rather at certain key points in the process.

All significant assessments are recorded. Exactly how this is done is at the discretion of the teams but the methods have to be consistent with three principles.

1. The assessments are compatible with the learning directed aims and the assessment scales.
2. Clear judgements are made in relation to these scales.
3. However briefly, the evidence on which the judgements are made is noted.

As mentioned in chapter 8, some joients are designed mainly for assessment purposes. These are normally quite short, lasting one session or less. They still have pupil-directed aims but the learning-directed aims are replaced by those that are assessment - directed. Though pupils may still be involved in some group activities the design of the joient ensures that all pupils have an opportunity to demonstrate their individual level of achievement on the chosen assessment scales. One example might be that the group completes a collection of maps, drawn to scale and with correct orientation, showing how to reach the school from different streets in the catchment area. Though pupils could combine to share their unassessed knowledge of street names, landmark buildings etc., they would each have to draw a map from the starting point nearest their home without assistance so as to assess their understanding of scale and orientation.

Such assessment joients are usually placed at or near the start of a school year or stage, to gauge where pupils are at and what their potential is. That these are necessary in no way implies that the planning team are ignoring the levels of achievement as recorded in the previous year's profiles. Indeed, what these show will be one factor in deciding the details of the joient. But it is a fact that pupils can regress, and progress, during school holidays. Also, even over a relatively short period, pupils' cognitive and other faculties mature. For example they are capable of running faster, developing more abstract arguments and concentrating for longer. Assessment joients, therefore, do not just check that previous learning has been retained or extended but test for greater potential learning. Organisations such as the CEM Centre at Durham University already use tests of this kind as a basis for comparison with later public examination results. Suitably modified to match the joient curriculum framework, they could be used by schools for the similar purpose of judging progress in relation to capability. Assessing against all the assessment scales is more elaborate than necessary and too time consuming. Normally, to limit the amount of this kind of testing, assessment joients are restricted to checking pupils' achievement and progress on the fundamental elements of the framework.

All joients require some kind of terminal assessment. In many, this can be done in the closing stages of the time allocated to the joient as the final part of the ongoing assessment through observation, listening and questioning. In the booklet example, practitioners can assess on-screen during the last or penultimate session the (hopefully), near-finished product rather than the final printed version. However, it is not always possible for practitioners to make a final assessment of some kinds of writing until the joient is complete. In a broadly similar joient to the example given, perhaps a class termly magazine, but undertaken by older pupils, the amount of writing involved might be too lengthy to permit accurate assessment during the time allocated to the joient. Such pieces of writing require marking in the traditional way out of lesson time. But the amount of writing that needs marking in this way is relatively small. Poetry, speeches and presentation texts can be mainly assessed through listening. Play scripts are best assessed through performance. Some writing, such as the recording of scientific experiments, requires only fairly brief checking for clarity and accuracy. Other pieces of writing, such as history, politics and philosophy essays or literary criticism require more detailed and time-consuming attention. It is possible to do some of this marking during the school day but on occasion practitioners need to devote evenings or weekends to this work. However, the burden for practitioners of this kind of marking is vastly reduced in comparison with existing practice because it is only required when written outcomes of a joient are the only or clearly the best way of judging achievement.

An important new feature of joient assessment is the assessment of groups as well as individuals. Group assessment is invariably based on the joients' pupil-directed aims, in the booklet example, the overall quality of the booklet and whether it was completed to the deadline. The different groups want and need to know how well they have done, particularly in competitive situations. Assessment of group performance can include reference to the strong or weak contributions made to its overall achievement by individuals within the group. Feedback to pupils on the achievement of groups is normally the final part of a joient. Occasionally, when the team planners need to 'reserve judgement', the feedback is immediately before the start of the next joient.

All joients, other than the assessment joients, include some degree of pupil and group self and/or peer assessment. The form that these assessments take varies widely according to the age of the pupils and the nature of the joient but they are always present even if in an attenuated form. Part of practitioners' assessments of individual pupils is based on the quality of pupils' assessment of themselves and others. Pupils' tendency, for example to under-rate or over-rate their own or others' performances, is related to an element of the personal, social and emotional development area of learning. In the booklet example, pupils within each group might usefully evaluate their own contribution and that of their peers, and each group within the class could evaluate the quality of the booklets produced by the other groups. It is part of the preliminary planning by the practitioners to decide how this should be undertaken, whether pupils should be allowed free range to air their views or be required to base them on criteria set by the teachers: 'how successful were the photographs in providing a fair picture of the school?' or 'was the text written in a way that new pupils would understand and set out in a way they would find helpful?'

Assessment by partners, such as governors, community leaders and the like, is also an important, though not a universal part of assessment. However, where partners have been heavily involved in planning a joient or in helping to implement it, they need also to be involved in its assessment in as far as practical considerations allow. Possibly in the booklet example a professional or good amateur photographer might have talked to the pupils in the preparatory stages about how to compose shots. His or her views on the outcomes would add authority and validity to the assessment.

Parents are probably the most important partners. Notwithstanding the vast differences in the way that they respond to being part of their children's learning and assessment, the principle of their involvement is one to which all schools and practitioners must adhere. Parents therefore need to be involved in providing assessment evidence. This often relates to the personal social and emotional area of learning. It is important to take into account how pupils behave outside the school and how parents perceive their children's progress. This is not done, as in the current system in some schools, as a parental comment on a completed report, but as part of the process of reaching final assessments.

So far, the assessment segments have been considered solely in relation to the joient programme. But there is another, sizeable, segment based on components of the third sessions such as outdoor activities and community service as described in chapter 10. This assessment is rather different. It is less formal; it is not necessarily based on the elements of the curricular framework, though some assessments may be. It contributes more, therefore, to the broader Record of Achievement (ROA) than to the Pupil Profile based on the assessment scales. Pupils and partners play a more dominant role. Pupils' self-assessment is taken at face value, though it may be moderated by practitioners. Partners' assessment is central in such components as community work, sporting and specialised physical individualised and group activities such as rock-climbing and rowing. The recording of achievements arising from the third session, and from out-of-school activities, is contained in the second part of the Record of Achievement, the first part being the Pupil Profile based on achievement and progress arising from the joients. The third and most slender part of the ROA lists results in external tests, which form the next segment.

In the joient system, the necessity for external national testing is greatly reduced, as is its value, to the point where it might be considered altogether superfluous. However, it is necessary for fair testing not only to be done but to be seen to be done. Those responsible for implementing the joient system need to be accountable to the nation. Government and others need reassurance that the joient system as a whole is resulting in pupils' achievement in line with the standards expected and that the level of individual pupils' achievements in the key learning elements is accurately stated. To that end there has to be a small amount of external assessment. There are various possible ways for this to be achieved. What follows is not the only, perhaps not the best, way but certainly a vast improvement on the current, over-blown system. Universal national testing is restricted to checking pupils' levels of achievement in the fundamental elements of the curriculum, such as basic literacy, numeracy, and their equivalents in the other main areas of learning. This testing only needs to occur at key points in pupils' education. One of these, definitely, is the point at which they leave full-time school education. Another, probably, is when they move from the primary to the secondary phase.

Important though it is that the nation in general is able to check whether pupils are meeting expectations and matching their peers in basic learning, it is also important for those professionally involved in the education system to have a broader external check on levels achieved in the other elements of the curriculum. To achieve this through universal testing would be to recreate a vast examination and testing industry, but universal testing is unnecessary. Sample testing across the whole curriculum is sufficient.

The principles for applying universal fundamental element testing and sample testing of other elements are straightforward. All pupils of the chosen age-group sit a single test on pre-determined dates; it may be necessary to run the test over two sessions. The test covers the whole curriculum. Most of the questions are common for all pupils, but a small number are different. Assuming for the sake of illustration a sample of 5% and a test consisting of ten questions spread over two sessions, eight of the questions are common to all pupils; two, each sampling a different element of learning, are different for each pupil in a group of forty. Pupils' individual levels of achievement are based only on the common questions. These levels, linked to the assessment scales of the national curriculum framework, are recorded in the third section of the Record of Achievement. They provide a quick preliminary check for potential employers and gatekeepers to further education. The sample questions are used solely for the purposes of obtaining a general picture.

All the test questions are the same nationwide. All the questions are marked regionally, but the answers to the sample questions are collated nationally. The questions are framed in the form that is familiar to pupils from the joient learning, that is to say that they are formulated as problems to be solved or challenges to be met. It is not enough for pupils to demonstrate that they have a particular skill; they must show that they can choose the right skill and apply it appropriately to a given situation. Questions are not necessarily concerned with a single area of learning and may, for example, include both literacy and numeracy, but they are devised so that the levels of literacy and numeracy can be separately assessed.

Passing mention has been made throughout this chapter to the Record of Achievement (ROA). It is the key document that follows pupils throughout their school careers. It retains its unique identity though, like the human body, while retaining the essential features of head, limbs etc., the constituent parts are constantly renewed and developed. The methods by which schools translate their own internal records into the ROA is their decision but the format and general contents of the ROA is standard across the system. Schools have to update it regularly, normally termly. It provides the basis for all contacts that practitioners and schools have with parents, employers and gatekeepers, as well as with the pupils themselves. A review tutorial based on the ROA is held, at least twice a year, involving parents and carers as well as pupils. These are not necessarily held *en masse* at parents evenings, though this remains a possibility, but can occur at mutually agreed times. The traditional written reports are no longer required. Tutors are responsible for ensuring that ROA are kept up to date and conform to the required standards. As with other parts of practitioners' role, their work in this area is subject to checking, internally by heads of house and externally by visiting moderators.

Chapter 12

Educational Superstructure

Cutting the educational ship of state down to size – school boards – local networks – regional boards – CAAT – Ministry of Schools and Settings – HMI – practitioner training

The ship of education in the late 20th and early 21st century is reminiscent of King Henry VIII's battleship, the Mary Rose, mentioned in an earlier chapter. This was a mighty and powerful vessel of great potential, but became progressively overloaded with an ever-increasing superstructure that ultimately, and notoriously, led to its capsizing and sinking into the Solent. HMS Education UK has not quite reached tipping point but the superstructure is in urgent need of reduction. This is what takes place in the joient system.

Before describing the new superstructure it is worth emphasising what has been swept away. Those organisations that have wholly vanished include Ofsted and school inspection agencies, local education authorities, examination boards and discrete teacher training departments. Those that remain but in reduced or modified form are a slimmed down central government ministry concerned with school education – its name is immaterial – HMI and QCA. It is, of course, a favourite ploy of governments, recorded as far back as the Roman Empire, to indulge in reorganisation so as to give the impression of being active, particularly when lacking any ideas for useful reform. Such reorganisations, despite often being dressed up as cost-cutting exercises, are expensive in time, money and expertise and usually achieve little. The reality is often little different after the organisation than it was before and all too often the new bureaucracies end up more bloated and less efficient than their predecessors. I am, therefore, all too conscious of the risks and costs of reorganisation, but nevertheless in this instance regard the risks as worth taking and the cost worth incurring in order to have a superstructure that builds logically on the new joient curriculum and which cuts out organisations that have outlived their usefulness. To guard against the dangers of bloated bureaucracy, the proposed organisations, which are described in more detail below, contain very few full-time bureaucrats or educational professionals not in regular contact with pupils. The dividing line between educational official and school practitioner is blurred. The distinction lies in what role a person is engaged in, not on who they are. This closer relationship should be mutually beneficial to both officialdom and school practice, helping to avoid the 'ivory tower syndrome' to which the former is prone and the sense of exclusion from shaping their own professional life that practitioners often feel.

In keeping with the joient system's bottom-up philosophy the description of the new, lightweight, superstructure begins at the lowest level of the new HMS Education: the schools themselves, as the engine room of the educational ship and the most important element in driving learning forward. As with the upper levels of the superstructure, the schools' bureaucracy is reduced, as already described in chapter 10, by division into mini-schools and semi-autonomous houses with a flat management structure.

Each school is governed by a widely representative school board wielding discretionary powers within the national legislative framework. Boards have powers to raise money as well as responsibility for making a budget and monitoring expenditure. They appoint heads of school and assist in the appointment of other senior staff. They are actively involved in developing the joient programme. They act very much as a board of directors, with the head of school as the chief executive.

The next level up is an informal one, consisting of networks of local schools, coming together to share expertise, develop joient programmes and liaise generally. These networks have no formal powers or responsibilities but receive official recognition and modest funding to encourage co-operation. Much of their networking is carried out using ICT but also involves periodic face-to-face meetings.

The next level, and the main driving forces of the joient system other than the schools themselves, consists of the regional boards. These are the regional arms of the national Curriculum, Accreditation, Assessment and Training (CAAT) board, the successor to QCA. As the title implies these regional boards have a range of responsibilities:

- developing joient programmes to reflect regional characteristics;
- accrediting school joient programmes;
- moderating school implementation of its joient programmes, assessment and recording procedures, tutorial arrangements and ROAs;
- administering and marking national tests, and informing schools and individual pupils in the region of their results;
- completing the training of new practitioners, the retraining of existing practitioners during the transitional period and providing continuing professional development for all practitioners, including management training for senior staff.

The boards consist of widely representative regional governing councils and a relatively small number of full-time professional staff, supported by administrative and secretarial staff. The majority of board members are part-time; experienced practitioners with proven expertise either on secondment or working part-time in schools and part-time for the board. They undertake the bulk of the regional board's outreach work as moderators, visiting advisers and trainers. They also assist the full-time professional staff with accreditation of joient programmes and the marking of national tests of essential elements. Because the same people are involved in this wide range of activities, schools do not get 'mixed messages' from organisations responsible for different aspects of educational provision.

Modern communication technology allows much of the board's work to be done without physical meetings. Nevertheless some face-to-fact contact is needed. Regional board HQs are therefore situated in locations which the vast majority of the region's schools can reach in less than two hours' travelling.

The national headquarters of the CAAT, which also needs to be located so that it is accessible from all the regions, contains a small body of highly skilled and experienced education professionals in its default state, but with the right and responsibility to employ a much larger group of professionals on short-term contracts when necessary, especially in the early stages of developing and implementing the joient system. Its role is similar to that of the electronic management system in modern cars, ensuring that intentions of the driver, that is the government as indicated in its policy decisions, are implemented efficiently by the 'working parts', the regional boards and schools. CAAT looks therefore to central government for strategic guidance and discusses with government the implications of its policy intentions and any potential difficulties arising from these. It also looks to its regional boards, monitoring the efficiency of their working and listening to feedback from them on the actual operation of the system. It has overall responsibility for the national testing, setting the questions for the national tests and overseeing the regional boards' marking. It also has responsibility for collating, analysing and publishing the national statistics.

At the top of the superstructure and suitably lightweight is the Department or Ministry of Schools and Settings consisting of ministers and three main branches.[1] The ministry's responsibilities cover all educational organisations up to the end of compulsory schooling. The difference between compulsory schooling and compulsory education is discussed in part 3.

At the heart of the ministry is the policy section. Its role is to develop, review and modify policy as necessary. The second section is concerned with finance, ensuring that the funding is divided in due proportion between schools in line with current policies for school funding, also that the CAAT HQ and regional boards, and the local school networks, are suitably funded.

The third branch is concerned with quality assurance and is the responsibility of HMI. HMI have three main roles. The first is to monitor the operation of the joient system as a whole, including the effectiveness of the lower levels of the superstructure. The second is to enable weakly performing schools to recover. This, as now, is tackled through regular visits and the setting of time-limited action plans. The identification of weak schools is not through inspection but by means of its results and feedback provided by moderators, advisers, and school boards; also through school self-evaluation. HMI's third responsibility is to carry out national surveys of particular aspects of the joient system as requested by the government, usually related to recent changes in policy.

In addition to these three main branches is one small section, consisting solely of administrators, with responsibility for independent schools. The place of the independent sector in the joient system is considered in the next chapter. Whatever the quality

---

[1] It is an organisational matter for government whether central government of schools and settings is the responsibility of a stand-alone ministry or part of a larger department that has other duties. Gordon Brown's recent decision to combine responsibilities for schools, families and children in a single department appears to make good organisational sense, provided that schools and settings continue to have their own ministers and civil servants and a duly proportionate share of central government funding.

assurance arrangements for independent schools, the Ministry still needs to administer their registration, and where necessary deregistration.

The demise of discrete teacher training departments in universities and other higher education organisations and the transfer of training to regional boards does not divorce higher education wholly from the education of teachers. Universities, as self-governing bodies, are still able to offer degrees in education as they wish but these need to cover a wide curricular range for at least part of courses designed to lead on to qualified teacher or practitioner status. The need for teachers with subject specialist knowledge remains, but such subject specialist knowledge, though still necessary, is no longer sufficient. The pedagogic training required becomes integrated with all other aspects of school education. Regional boards take responsibility for turning those with education degrees into effective classroom practitioners in partnership with schools. Most of the pedagogic training takes place where it is most logically placed, in the schools themselves. Most schools, and many planning teams within them, have at least one practitioner in training, working alongside the teams and moving progressively from observation to fully integrated working with the team. Regional boards and senior staff within schools share responsibility for monitoring the work of practitioners in training. Final accreditation lies with the regional board. The length of the probationary period is flexible and depends on the rate at which the practitioner progresses but is never less than a full school year.

Chapter 13

Special Features

Ethnic minority groups – special educational needs and physical disability – learning difficulties – behavioural problems – independent schools

The preceding chapters in part 2 have provided outline maps of the whole joient system in general terms. The system is intended to apply across the whole range of schools and pupil abilities, for it is one of the fundamental aims of the joient system to provide for pupils of all kinds of abilities and attitudes, including especially what was earlier described as the hard core of poorly motivated pupils. Nevertheless, no single system can cope with all situations unless some adjustments are made. The special features considered in this chapter vary widely and require different solutions. They are concerned with particular groups of pupils, and with particular aspects of the curriculum and school ownership. What is offered here is no more than a sketch map. There is no pretence at a comprehensive consideration of all the issues involved, for each area is a complex one requiring specialist knowledge. Pupils with special needs, for instance, have widely divergent problems and needs. All this page of the Atlas seeks to do is to give a general idea of how the education of these various groups of pupils can be accommodated within the joient system.

It is best to start with those groups of pupils whose needs the joient system can absorb most easily. The needs of ethnic minority groups, leaving aside any specific language or other learning skills that they may have, can be identified and met through the school joient programme to ensure that their cultural traditions are recognised and included.

The active learning approach of the joient system also increases the likelihood of improving boys' poor motivation, which has been identified as one of the reasons for their less good performance than girls in public examinations. The greatly enhanced tutorial system assists schools to monitor and remediate any lack of progress in those areas, such as language development, where boys tend towards lack of commitment. Research evidence suggests that the difference between boys and girls is in their disposition to learn rather than their capacity to do so. In certain areas of learning and at certain ages, boys require more external pressure than girls to learn. Insofar as girls have educational needs, these mainly lie in lack of self-confidence in areas of learning such as mathematics and physics. These needs appear to be declining as girls and women have become more assertive and successful. Where they still remain, the tutorial system, combined with care taken over pupil grouping, can provide the necessary confidence.

A significant proportion of pupils have medium-term or long-term special needs relating to both physical disability and learning difficulties. Because these range so widely in severity and nature, a wide spectrum of solutions is necessary.

Great advances have been made in understanding and providing for the needs of pupils with physical disabilities. Specialised schools remain essential for those with severe problems such as profound deafness. For those with moderate difficulties, specialist units attached to mainstream schools are the best solution, enabling disabled pupils to join with their mainstream peers whenever practicable and receive specialist support when this is not the case. The general features of the joient system with regard to joint working, curricular programmes, assessment and recording apply equally to these pupils. Pupils with mild disabilities can operate in mainstream schools with only occasional modifications to their programmes but may require full-time or part-time carers to overcome problems of mobility. The best practice currently evident for these pupils can be carried forward into the joient system and further developed as technological innovations increasingly provide solutions to circumvent their disabilities.

Very much the same applies to pupils with learning difficulties. They too, depending on the extent of their difficulties, require specialist schools, attached units or additional support in mainstream schools. The greater recognition given to different kinds of ability means that pupils with special needs in one area of learning, such as writing, will have greater opportunities to do well in other areas, thus boosting their overall confidence and motivation. The concept of 'special needs pupils' being a class apart disappears.[1]

The joient system provides plentiful opportunities for gifted and talented pupils to reach their potential and to develop their particular talents to a high level through the third session components. However, it does so without removing them from the mainstream groups; it requires them to develop their learning across the whole curriculum and to increase their awareness of those areas where they are perhaps relatively weak.

Pupils with behavioural difficulties pose a challenge for the joient system, involving as it does a greatly increased amount of group work and self-discipline. A simplistic but useful distinction can be made between pupils whose behaviour results from 'nurture' and those

---

[1] It has recently been suggested that the aim should be to regard all pupils having some form of special need. In principle, this is right. Given that no two people are exactly alike, their learning needs will always differ, even if only in subtle ways. The principle, therefore, should be that 'all pupils are special'; the practical implications of this are formidable

where it is a consequence of 'nature'. Some pupils' anti-social behaviour derives from inadequate parenting and harsh social and economic circumstances. Where these continue through pupils' school years, changing their behaviour for the better will always remain problematic. Nevertheless, since their behavioural characteristics are not inherent in their personalities but the result of their experiences, it is reasonable to believe that what has been done to them can be undone. Providing a strong alternative ethos where co-operation is emphasised and rewarded offers some hope that such pupils can escape from the vicious circle of emotional, social and economic deprivation which they have experienced out of school.

A different challenge is posed by those whose behavioural problems are innate, with conditions such as autism and Asperger's syndrome. Such pupils have limited potential for co-operative behaviour and may disrupt other pupils' learning in groups while making little progress themselves. The problem is essentially a medical or psychological one rather than a social one and it can only be hoped that advances in medical science will lead to cures or at least a reduction in the symptoms associated with these conditions. In the meanwhile schools need to make case-by-case decisions on how these pupils can best be provided for.

Only one subject within the areas of learning poses a special difficulty. This is religious education, and it is only a difficulty because of the existence of faith schools. As in any other set of schools some faith schools are excellent; most are at least acceptable and a few are terrible. The issue is not one of quality but of the confusion that arises between religious education – a proper concern for all schools – and religious instruction in a particular faith. A modern Solomon, with his power and wisdom, would remove faith schools from the educational highway, but allow them time, Friday to Sunday as appropriate to the religion, for religious instruction (RI). Since no such scenario seems remotely likely given the still powerful position that the churches have in Britain, some kind of compromise is needed. Religious education (RE) has its due place within the national curriculum framework and all schools, of whatever faith or no faith, are equally obliged to pay heed to them and are equally subject to accreditation and moderation. Schools that wish to offer religious instruction must make a clear distinction between RI and RE. These must occur at different times. In order not to breach the principle of due proportion, schools offering RI need to use either the contingency time within the first two sessions or some of the time in the third session.

Schools in the independent sector can choose between co-existence with the joient system or co-operation with it. In the world context, the concept of 'independence' varies widely. Historically, the independence of English schools has been far greater than those in many other countries. However, a recent and continuing trend has been towards ever closer government regulation and the very concept of independence is coming under government scrutiny. Whether governmental control of independent schools will ultimately include tight prescription of the curriculum remains unclear. What follows is based on the assumption that the government will not make such substantial changes to the current regulations that independent schools will be unable to plan and implement their own curricula.

The disappearance of national tests and external examinations at 16 is of little concern to independent schools as many choose not to participate in the tests and place much more weight on post-16 examinations than the current GCSE. Because the vast majority of independent secondary schools have sixth-forms and see as one of their chief aims the preparation of pupils for university education they are little concerned with achievement at 16. Should they wish to continue with external assessment for younger age-groups, systems that measure progress between set ages already exist and are widely used. It is likely that the international GCSE, also used by some, will continue for British-style schools overseas and therefore still be available. With the abolition of Ofsted and school inspections in the maintained sector, it is probable that independent schools will also wish to discontinue external inspections other than those required to ensure that they meet regulations. Currently the independent schools inspectorate (ISI) inspects those schools in membership of associations that make up the Independent Schools Council (ISC) while HMI inspect the remainder, focusing primarily on compliance with regulations. It would be for government and the ISC to agree on quality assurance arrangements but logical for a single body to have responsibility for all independent schools.

If independent schools as a body, or individual schools, decide to participate in the joient system, they may not legally have to abide by the rules of accreditation, moderation and assessment by CAAT regional boards but can choose to do so. They are also able to opt out of the national tests as these do not provide information of value to them or to national policy makers. As to the long-term position of the independent sector, what it does and the proportion of pupils that it educates will depend largely on the perception of schools and their potential parents of the joient system's success. If it proves successful, an increasing number of parents may choose the less costly option of the maintained system. Nevertheless, even if the gap in investment per pupil between the independent and the maintained sector narrows, it remains likely that many independent schools will continue to offer a richer curriculum, particularly in the third session choice, and more favourable staffing ratios than maintained schools can afford. These attractions, along with the cachet of private education that will subside only slowly given its high reputation and the weight of tradition, make it likely that the independent sector will maintain a retain a significant proportion of the education market and continue to reduce the cost to the taxpayer of the maintained system.

Part 3: Getting There

Chapter 14

Prelude: A Moses Moment

Getting to the promised land – phases in the journey: curriculum development, staff retraining, transitional arrangements

Having come so far, approaching 30,000 words to date in this work and having spent some four decades trekking purposefully but with mixed emotions through what, very often, was an educational wilderness, I am gladdened by the vision of the future of English education, however blurred and incomplete, that my experience has afforded me. I am also saddened at the prospect that I may not live to see and enter the Promised Land of the joient system, despite some recent signs that others well placed in education are already starting to share my vision. I find myself, therefore, empathising with Moses, as he stood on Mount Nebo and looked down on the land flowing with milk and honey, knowing that he would not reach it. Though it was left to Joshua actually to lead the Israelites to the promised land, Moses no doubt advised him on how to get there. The third part of this Atlas, therefore, describes what needs to be done to make the joient system a reality and how obstacles may be overcome. The way is not smooth but it is passable with determination and clear sightedness.

The introductory period for the joient system divides naturally into three phases, which are considered in detail in the next three chapters:
1. Laying the foundations of the system, in particular developing the curricular framework.
2. Re-training the practitioners. This is massive in scale and more psychologically than technically difficult, requiring practitioners to accept the need for change and appreciate the merits of the new system.
3. The period of transition, actually moving from the old maps to the new without putting at risk the education of pupils caught up in the change.

The introductory period as a whole is likely to last about five years. Many schools will probably complete their implementation at least a year earlier than this. It will be open for schools to make a start on both the re-training and implementation before the formal beginnings of these phases. As always with major changes, there are both advantages and disadvantages in being 'ahead of the game'. Having longer to prepare eases the pressures and stresses of change. However, late changes to the curricular framework and the re-training policies may require some re-learning or modification of the training or implementation strategies.

Chapter 15

Developing the Curricular Framework

Key role of the coordinating committee – the 12 stages of development

Before the curricular framework can be developed, the key organisations need to be established and key people appointed. This is described is some detail – a more detailed map than those preceding it – for a good reason. The original National Curriculum was flawed, not because of any failure on the part of those charged with putting – or should one say – cobbling it together, but because the development process was misconceived. The original curriculum had to be expensively reviewed and re-vamped by Lord Deering. He did a good rescue job but what emerged was a fudge nevertheless. The development process for the joient system has to be designed to avoid any possibility of repeating former mistakes.

The first step is for the government to appoint a chairman and chief executive of CAAT, the body that will bring the curricular framework into existence. Once appointed, CAAT, in addition to setting up its own core staff and working procedures, needs to initiate the process of developing the framework in a series of stages as set out below.

Stage 1a   CAAT appoints the framework coordinating committee. This body has the prime responsibility for overseeing the development of the framework and for its final version.

The composition of this group is vital to the success of the whole enterprise. Individually its members must have the highest expertise in curricular matters and a proven record in taking a broad and balanced view of education, not a strong particularist line. Members need to be drawn from schools, higher education, further education, business and other professions. Collectively they need to be familiar with all the areas of learning. As a body, the coordinating committee needs to be tough and businesslike with a strong chairman.

Stage 1b Government appoints a steering committee to oversee the CAAT's work during the development stages. This should include HMI.

Stage 2 The coordinating committee, taking advice as necessary, sets up subject groups to define fundamental and desirable elements for the curricular framework and accompanying assessment framework. Suggested nominations for the groups come mainly from the subject associations, using the word 'subject' in the broadest sense. Members of subject groups also need to be drawn from schools, further and higher education, business and the relevant professions. The religious education group needs to be drawn from all Britain's major faiths; also from atheists and humanists. The coordinating committee sets out the criteria that the group proposals must satisfy, and groups are left in no doubt that these cannot be ignored. These criteria lay down the maximum number of fundamental and desirable elements. They stipulate that all aspects of learning must be considered, including attitudes/actions as well as skills, knowledge and understanding; and they set down the number of points required for the assessment scales.

Stage 3 Each subject group draws up its draft proposals for the fundamental and desirable elements and submits these to the coordinating committee for provisional approval. It also produces a draft set of assessment scales.

DEVELOPING THE CURRICULAR FRAMEWORK

Stage 4   The coordinating committee considers all the draft proposals, either accepting them or requiring them to be modified. At this stage the task of the committee is only to ensure that the each of the proposals meets the criteria. Dealing with the detail and issues of overlap or duplication between groups come later. For any set of proposals that do not meet the criteria, the subject groups concerned are required to reconsider and resubmit.

Stage 5a   Once the subject group draft proposals are approved, they are put out for wide-ranging consultation. This should be a genuine consultation process with a realistic time-scale for receiving and considering the responses.

Stage 5b   During the consultation period, CAAT sets up its regional boards and makes senior staff appointments. These consist of regional directors and heads of the phase sections from lower primary to upper secondary. Regional senior staff begin the process of identifying and appointing part-time staff, initially to design joient programmes.

Stage 5c   Also during the consultation period, the coordinating committee commissions a small working group of its members, who may co-opt others, to undertake two tasks. The first is to start putting together the draft curriculum framework, collating identical or similar elements proposed by different committees and repeating the process for assessment. These are complex and time-consuming tasks and likely to require going back to subject committees where the working group proposes significant modifications.

Stage 6   Subject groups revise their draft proposals taking into account the responses to the consultation and comments from the coordinating committee's working group; they submit a final proposal to the coordinating committee.

Stage 7   In the light of the final proposals, the working group modifies its draft curriculum and assessment frameworks as necessary and presents a final draft curricular framework to the coordinating committee for consideration and, after any further modification, final approval.

Stage 8: The proposed curriculum framework, and accompanying assessment scales, are published, mainly to inform the educational world of the proposals but also to allow for a short period of final consultation.

Stage 9 Subject to any last-minute fine-tuning and comments by the steering group, the framework is submitted for ratification by government and for the initiation of any necessary legislation. (The legal processes that may need to be set in motion are not considered here. Currently there is such a plethora of Education Acts and legislations that it would be tedious to analyse and set out what legislative changes are needed. Hopefully a single act, sweeping away those earlier provisions that are no longer relevant, will provide the legislative foundation for the joient system.)

Stage 10 Once government agrees the framework, the coordinating committee working group develops sample joients to act as exemplars, initially for regional boards and subsequently for schools.

Stage 11 Having regard to the sample joients, but also drawing on the expertise of its staff, the regional boards design a complete joient programme for each of the educational phases, submitting them to CAAT HQ for approval.

Stage 12 Once approved, the regional boards publish their joient programmes and begin the process of assisting schools to devise their own.

This concludes the development of the curricular framework and leads on to the development of school joient programmes. Stage 11 is a long one and runs in parallel with the practitioner training programme that is the subject of the next chapter.

Two things are important throughout the 12 stages. The first is that they should not be rushed. CAAT must resist political pressure to steamroller the proposals through. All involved will be on a sharp learning curve. Sufficient time needs to be available for early mistakes to be realised and rectified and for as much of the devilry in the detail as possible to be sorted out in the curricular development phase, while accepting that some modifications may prove to be necessary in the light of the experience of implementing the joient system in the pilot phase. The second point is that the coordinating committee must at all times be in charge and driving the proposals forward, even if it meets with strong opposition from some quarters.

It might be argued that for each regional board to create a complete set of joients is inefficient and that it would be better for a single set to be devised by CAAT HQ staff. Defining efficiency narrowly in the sense of the amount of time collectively devoted by the staff involved, this is unarguably true; but this is an instance of where the long-term effectiveness of the joient system is more important than short-term efficiency in the development phase.

There are a number of strong reasons for devising several sets of joients. One is that a single set would create the impression that a national curriculum had been re-invented. Having regional variations dispels that impression, both symbolically and in reality. A second reason is that the existence of several sets of joients allows schools to choose what suits them best, to opt for one regional set or, more likely, to 'pick and mix'. A third reason is that as many people as possible with a high level of expertise should be involved in the development of joients. The later phases of development require the dissemination to schools of experience in joient design. For practical reasons the pool of experienced joient designers needs to be large enough for the dissemination process to take place without undue delays.

Chapter 16

Re-training the Practitioners

Winning minds and hearts – three elements of retraining: explanatory, cognitive and experiential – involvement of parents, partners and pupils

In many ways the re-training of practitioners is the most crucial and the most difficult part of the process. The practical challenges of re-training a complete workforce of many thousands while they continue to do their jobs are formidable. Equally formidable is the task of persuading the practitioners that this is a change to be welcomed. Hopefully they will appreciate that the advantages for them of the new system will outweigh the anxieties always associated with major change and the inevitable losses.

The greatest challenge is to win over the out-and-out subject specialist teachers at secondary level as they have most to lose and most to re-learn. Primary-trained practitioners and those in secondary schools more concerned with development of pupils in the round or with courses rather than subjects are likely to find adjustment to the new system much easier and are more likely to favour the new approach.

There is a tough message for any teachers whose objections are along the lines of "I came into teaching to teach my subject.". Subject expertise is a valuable means to that end but not an end in itself. The key concept of the joient system from the point of view of practitioners is that the planning teams are very largely responsible for advancing the learning of their groups of pupils across the whole curriculum. Practitioners have to come to terms with the fact that they do not always have as much subject-specialised expertise as they would like. They need to accept the idea that, as educated people themselves, they should possess expertise across a fair, if not complete, range of areas of learning at a level above that which their pupils are expected to achieve. (This is, of course, a commonplace already for primary teachers). They may also need to learn how to access necessary specialist expertise through making use of others within their own school, in the local school networks and by tapping into the vast array of information that the world wide web provides. Additionally, they need to become more accustomed to working more flexibly and in small teams, without the previous comfort zones of fixed weekly timetables and subject syllabuses that change little from year to year.

The changes, while potentially stressful, are exciting. Though it cannot be more than an informed guess, my optimistic belief is that the overwhelming majority of teachers, once they have understood the system and its merits, will relish the challenge and the return to doing a job that requires real professionalism rather than jumping through the hoops positioned and frequently re-positioned by others, which has increasingly been their fate in the last four decades.[1]

The re-training of existing practitioners has three necessary elements. The first is explanatory; the second is cognitive; the third is experiential.

Explaining the system takes many forms. The consultation processes described in the previous chapter raises awareness of what is involved amongst those who participate in the consultation or who

---

[1] Anyone who has read Lewis Carroll's *Alice* books will be struck by the similarity between the plight of teachers and that of Alice on the Queen of Hearts's croquet lawn.

keep in touch with it. The publication of the framework and the sample joients assists all practitioners in acquiring a feel for the practical implications. However, the explanations most likely to be persuasive are those provided by fellow practitioners on the basis of their first-hand experience. To this end, from as early a stage as possible, schools such as Telford that have already moved a good way down the road toward the joient system are encouraged to experiment, to pilot parts of the curriculum and to share their 'insider' understanding of the system, once it is finalised, with those schools that express most enthusiasm for it. These schools in turn form the second and larger wave of pilot schools. They too try out parts of the system and subsequently share their expertise with the generality of schools in their area. Regional boards are responsible for managing, facilitating, funding and contributing their own expertise to these explanatory sessions. Local geography and circumstances determine precisely how this training is delivered but ideally it is done through local school networks to emphasise from the start the importance of co-operation between schools and the sharing of both anxieties and expertise.

Also in the spirit of co-operation, the explanatory training needs to include parents, existing and potential partners, and the pupils themselves. They need training rather than mere raising of awareness as all will have an active part to play. It is important, therefore, that from an early stage they understand what the system involves and how their participation contributes to it.

Between completing the explanatory and undertaking the cognitive elements of their re-training, all practitioners are required to undertake self-evaluation of what they perceive their specific training needs to be. For many secondary and some primary teachers this may well lie in revising or extending experience and expertise in subject areas that they have not taught recently or at all. Universities and other higher education institutions have a key role to play in providing revision or extension courses in a range of curricular areas and at different levels appropriate to the different sub-phases. Most likely these will be delivered using distance learning packages.

Practitioners who need this kind of re-training receive reductions in their current teaching loads in order to undertake this study. Such provision cannot be afforded or managed in a hurry so this element of the training needs to run for a considerable period, probably two years, though the training courses themselves vary in length depending on the degree of need.

Whereas the curricular area training is individualised to meet the particular needs of each practitioner, all need training, to a varying extent, in the development of joients and the detailed planning for their implementation. This is achieved by 'on the job' training through developing and planning some of the actual joients that eventually form part of the school's joient programme. However, in the early stages, to avoid the situation of the 'blind leading the blind', pilot school staff are involved, along with regional board advisers, in inculcating the principles of good joient planning and implementation through case-study development, working with school network groups wherever practicable. As schools become more confident and proficient in applying these skills, the support is progressively withdrawn. Partners should be encouraged to join the training where practicable or at least kept informed about what is developing.

The third, experiential, element, leads on naturally from the second. It employs the strategies that have proved successful over the years for the induction of beginner teachers and involves the observation of trainers by trainees and vice-versa. Over a period of time all practitioners observe others more experienced as they implement a joient. In the early stages some school staff observe in pilot schools. They then develop and implement one or more joients in their own school, observed by a member of staff from a pilot school or a regional board adviser. Once confident and competent, these staff act as the trainers and observers for other staff in their own school. To make these observations and pilots possible during the period of re-training, the existing school curriculum and timetable has to be somewhat shrunk. Senior staff in schools will need to manage this. The time required for pupils working towards examinations under the previous system needs to be protected so that these pupils' interests are not harmed. For all other pupils, some reduction in the 'traditional' curriculum, given that it will be replaced by more worthwhile elements, will not be to their disadvantage. Schools need to keep their pupils and parents well informed about the changes that occur during the retraining, and the subsequent, transitional, phase.

Chapter 17

Managing the Transition

Phasing out the GCSE work – phasing in ROA – primary school flexibility – staffing review

There is no doubt that the period of transition from a system focused on subject-based external examinations to the joient system is the hardest part to achieve successfully. No major change comes costless. Some eggs have to be broken to achieve a tastier and more nutritious educational omelette. Whilst every effort has to be made to ensure that the education of those that occurs during the transitional period is not significantly harmed, it would be idle to pretend that it will be wholly unaffected. To minimise serious damage, this chapter sets out in some, perhaps tedious detail how the transition *might be* managed. Others might well come up with better arrangements. The point of this chapter, therefore, is to describe not what *has* to be done but what *could* be done to move to the new system. As for the assessment chapter, general readers may find the detail of the transition process somewhat excessive and may prefer to skim the chapter fairly lightly.

In line with the general philosophy of the joient system, it is for individual schools to decide how, in detail, they manage the transition. Their plans, however, need to stay within the overall framework and time-scales laid down by CAAT.

In order to minimise the disruption to the work of pupils working on GCSE or vocational diploma courses at 16, schools are obliged to continue with these courses for a minimum of two years and a maximum of three after the formal start of the implementation phase (I-day). The three-year span is to allow those schools that begin teaching GCSE courses in Year 9 to continue this arrangement for those pupils who are in Year 9 in the school year following I-day. Schools have discretion as to whether or not other Year 9 pupils continue to follow the existing Year 9 curriculum for one year and then take GCSEs or diploma courses. From I-day+1 year all Year 9 pupils have to follow the joient programme for the upper secondary stage and be assessed using national tests and Records of Achievement based on the work of at least three years. All pupils in Years 7 and 8 in the year following I-day start on the joient system and their ROA is based on a minimum of five and four years respectively.

Primary schools have the option to delay implementing the joient system for pupils who start Year 5 and Year 6 in the year following I-day but all other pupils start on the joient system immediately.

It is open to all schools to start introducing the joient system, probably in part, before I-day, either for certain areas of learning or for selected age groups. These age groups could include Years 10 and 11. Pupils in these transitional years are expected to take at least five GCSEs, including English and mathematics, but other subjects that they might have taken are replaced by joients that contain elements of these subjects. It is likely that most schools will start by using the joients provided by CAAT HQ and regional boards. If they wish to develop their own, they need to obtain accreditation from the regional boards. All schools need to introduce at least a small number of pilot joients into their curriculum as part of the retraining process described in the previous chapter.

Before I-day dawns, schools need to review their staffing arrangements so that their planning teams are defined, trained and have done the necessary planning for implementing joients before the deadline. This will pose few problems for primary schools, which are accustomed to working in year-group or Key Stage teams. For secondary schools, the staff need increasingly to be divided into lower or upper secondary in order to facilitate the formation of the planning teams. This does not necessarily mean that practitioners remain indefinitely within one sub-phase. While a single planning team normally remains responsible for the learning of its group through the complete sub-phase, it is for individual schools to decide whether these teams should 'move up' with their groups or remain within the sub-phase.

Schools vary in their particular staffing circumstances and in the way that they decide how to manage the transitional phase. It is undeniable that there will be difficulties, pressure points and some formidable challenges for managers and school timetablers. External support is necessary, particularly in the form of additional short-term staffing but also in terms of flexibility and understanding on the part of all those affected by the changes. Few, if any, schools will get everything right first time. It is crucial that they, and those at the various other levels of the superstructure, put across a balanced message, emphasising the real educational gains as well as the possible glitches in the early stages. Claiming too much too soon, as politicians are wont to do, only loses long-term general support. Prophesies of doom from the Cassandras and mutterings of the 'Old Guard' will no doubt continue to pour out and be sensationalised by certain elements in the media whenever a glitch occurs. The proponents and exponents of the joient system need to be aware that this will happen and have plans to counter it when it occurs.

Part 4: Unmapped territory

Chapter 18

"Here be Dragons"

Post-16 education – finance – history

The proposals set out in parts 2 and 3 are the end result of a long period of consideration. The maps may not be detailed; they may be neither entirely accurate nor convincing but they have been drawn with care. A wise author, particular one who bases his case on solid evidence drawn from long experience, would probably have concluded the book at this point, as indeed was my original intention. I realise that the decision to extend the book by entering a more speculative world is risky. Well-founded criticisms of the suggestions put forward in the next three chapters might be taken as undermining the validity of earlier arguments.

I decided, nevertheless, to pursue this risky course because the earlier part of the work demanded it. This may seem a strange statement but it is little different to those made by authors who claim that the characters that they invent take on lives of their own that demand to be told. In the process of drafting the first three parts, it seemed to be ever more necessary at least to consider some of the key issues arising from them and, in the modern information jargon, the 'frequently asked questions' (FAQ), to which readers might want answers.

Part 4 is therefore very different from those that precede it. Here, the ideas put forward are much more speculative and less fully worked out. The mapping, such as it is, is more akin to the efforts of medieval map-makers to fill with dragons and other mythical beasts the gaps that existed in unexplored territories than to any serious modern cartographical activity based on reliable evidence. Redefining the phases of education, which is the concern of the next chapter, emerged as a logical extension of the joient system. Thinking about how education can best be financed in the chapter that then follows also grew naturally from the chapters in part 3 dealing with the implementation of the joient system. The final chapter of this part, which indicates what the fundamental and some desirable elements might be for the subject of history, is rather different and more in the nature of an answer to FAQ. Though also tentative, it differs in being based more firmly on direct experience. It is a first and partial attempt at the kind of large-scale mapping that will eventually need to be produced for the whole terrain, but which will require the combined efforts of many visionary brains rather than a single, lone voice in the wilderness.

All three areas, educational phases, finance and history, though very different, have in common the fact that they are dragon country. Though there has been relatively little controversy about the age at which younger children change schools, nothing during the last half century has been more controversial, muddled and full of failures both in the doomed proposals and in the reality than post-16 education and its challenger, 14-18 education.

Attempting to propose anything reliable to do with the financing of government-owned or sponsored undertakings is highly risky. The forecasting of costs is a very inexact science, if indeed it can make any claim at all to be scientific. Projects such as The Dome and the Olympics spring immediately to mind.

All academics are quarrelsome and none more so than historians, for whom disagreement, sometimes acrimonious, is part of their way of life. To attempt therefore to sketch out proposals that would need general support from historians is indeed to enter the dragon's den.

It could be that the proposals in all three chapters are misconceived through ignorance, perverseness, naivity or all three. However, if these final maps in the Atlas are poor descriptors of the future reality that they seek to describe, it is worth repeating that this does not invalidate the proposals in the previous parts. Proposals in parts 2 and 3 could all be implemented without any of the changes proposed here. The three chapters in part 4 are intended to as no more than introductions to other areas of educational debate than those that have been the main focus of this work. They point to possible 'next steps' and suggest further mapping of the educational world that needs to be done.

Chapter 19

Compulsory Schooling and Compulsory Education –

Redefining the Phases

Redefining the phases of education – leaving school at 15 – compulsory education to 18 – broadening the assessment base – enhancing Further Education colleges

During the period in which this work has been drafted, a series of policy statements or intentions have emerged from government. While some involve no more than re-arranging Titanic's seating plan, a few are of real importance for the future. None more so than the realisation than compulsory schooling and compulsory education are not the same thing. Government now appears to accept that all young people should continue in education until the age of 18, but that this should not mean that the school leaving age is raised to 18: continuing education can be provided in other kinds of institutions and organisations. Similarly, government appears to be edging towards a position where all children are entitled to receive nursery education. Both of these developments are welcome and they prompt a reconsideration of what the phases of education should be and where they should take place.

Research evidence about the effects of education on younger children contains mixed messages. On the one hand, the value of nursery education is stressed; on the other, the effects of an early start to formal schooling are said to be damaging. England is unusual in starting formal education as early as 5. At the other end of the age-scale a debate has long raged between the advocates of the various forms of post-16 education and the champions of 14-18 education. Perhaps the time has come to re-think the phases of schooling. There is nothing sacrosanct, or rooted in development psychology, about the present ages of transfer from nursery to primary, primary to secondary, or secondary to further or higher education. Since young people mature at very different rates, it could hardly be otherwise.

I started this work with intention of proposing radically different ways of enabling pupils' learning using the existing educational framework. The reason for this was to avoid being marked down as a wild utopian lacking connection with the real world. I also hoped to avoid coming up with ideas that required yet more reorganisation of schools for reasons that were explained in part 1. However, I have increasingly found this self-imposed condition to be restrictive, and perhaps unnecessary. It may be that the new wine is best not contained in old wineskins.

The new proposed phase definitions are not, therefore, a necessary pre-condition for the introduction and success of the joient system but they would make it easier in some ways.

Though education is life-long, it is reasonable to accept that the state should not require its people to prolong their education beyond the age of 18 unless they wish to do so. It makes logical sense to divide these 18 years into three-year units, birth to 3, 3-6 and so on, and organisational sense to combine these into mainly six-year units. The first phase of education, which could be called the infant phase, though the titles are unimportant, is based in the home and lasts from 0-3. The second phase, the nursery phase, lasts from 3-6 and the third, the early-school phase, from 6-9. For organisational reasons the second and third phases can conveniently be grouped together in junior schools. Attendance would be required from age 3 but on a part-time basis and with a frequency dependent on a child's social, emotional and intellectual maturity. Compulsory full-time education would start from 6.

The fourth phase, middle school 9-12, and fifth phase, upper school 12-15, could also be conveniently grouped together to form senior schools. All pupils in the maintained sector would leave school at 15 to continue their compulsory further education primarily in college but with work placements for another three years as students 15-18. The existing school sixth forms would disappear.

At age 18, students could choose to stay on in college, either part-time, combined with employment, or full time in enhanced further education; or in higher education at first degree level, depending on their wishes and capabilities. Alternatively they could transfer to universities at this point. The notion of institutions combining sixth-form, further and higher education teaching is not without precedent. In the 1970s and 80s the Cambridge College of Arts and Technology (CCAT) taught with success students aged 16 to 21, offering A level and traditional first degree courses as well as a range of 'vocational courses'. Expanding the remit of Further Education colleges to include some higher education work would raise their profile and give more credibility to the present government's target of educating half the workforce to degree level.

The main difference between schools and colleges would be that all school pupils up to 15 followed a common curriculum whereas college students would have a degree of choice and the opportunity to slant their studies in a particular direction. Colleges, like schools, would follow the general principles of the joient system at least to 18. For the students aged 15-18, colleges would develop their curriculum in terms of joient programmes covering all the areas of learning. However, the definition of 'due proportion' would change to allow specialisation and choice. As in baccalaureate courses, all students would be required to continue their studies in all areas of learning, but with significantly different degrees of emphasis. Approximately half of their learning would be devoted to their non-specialist areas.

The other half would be concerned with their specialist studies. The range of choice could encompass two or more subjects at levels approximately equivalent to A level or the higher levels of the international baccalaureate. Equally they could focus on particular business or technical areas providing the equivalent of the first three years of an apprenticeship. The assessment and recording procedures would also be similar to those for schools. They would involve ROA, a limited range of national tests at 18 in essential skills that might resemble the American SAT reasoning tests (previously known as Scholastic Assessment Tests) and also nationally designed tests of achievement in the specialist areas such as automotive engineering or hotel and catering as well as single 'academic' subjects. This multiple assessment system would provide gatekeepers with a wide range of indicators to use in selecting students for higher education. As independent institutions, universities would continue to decide for themselves how they selected students but hopefully they would appreciate the advantages of being able to refer to different forms of assessment rather than rely on the existing outdated, unreliable and narrowly based system of A-level grades and points scores.

Defining the phases with an overlapping age, eg 6-9 and 9-12, is deliberate. It allows a measure of flexibility in the age at which pupils move between the stages. This reflects the fact that pupils mature and advance intellectually at different rates. In the normal course of events some pupils would, for example, move from junior to senior schools very shortly after their eighth birthday, while others would be nearly nine. Exceptionally, pupils might transfer from junior to senior schools at eight or ten. For all pupils, the decision would be taken on their ROA as a whole. For example, they would not transfer early just because they were intellectually advanced unless their personal, social and emotional development was also sufficiently developed to allow them to survive and thrive amongst older pupils. The same flexibility, and the same exceptional arrangements, would apply to the move from school to college, but the decision to delay transfer would need to be accepted by the individual students in those instances where their compulsory education would thereby be extended beyond the age of 18.

The main difference between universities and colleges would be that colleges would be wholly concerned with teaching whereas universities would continue to combine research with teaching and would offer higher degrees at masters and doctorate level as well as first degrees.

The implementation of the redefined stages would have cost implications for the school and college building stock. Remodelling schools for the revised age-ranges would take time. The lowering of the school leaving age to 15 would reduce the challenges of retraining the out-and-out subject specialist teachers. Those who preferred a subject emphasis in their work would transfer to colleges, where they would have the possibility of teaching their subjects or other specialisms up to first-degree level. Those who preferred the joient curriculum in the secondary phase would not need to raise their level of subject expertise to such a high level as would be required if the school leaving age remained at 16.

Chapter 20

Who Pays?

Static normal costs – increased development costs – central agency financial administration– school levy – charitable giving – local accountability

This page of the Atlas has the fewest features. The detail of finance is something that I instinctively try to avoid. Fortunately, there are many others who do not share my attitude and it will be for them to delight in working out the financial implications of the joient system. Those generally in support will find ways to demonstrate that the figures do add up and are affordable; doubters will figure out that the proposals are unaffordable. Such features as do appear in this chapter are less to do with numbers and more about who pays the piper and calls the tune.

There is no reason why the joient system, in its steady state, should cost any more than the present system of school education. Staffing, which makes up by far the largest single item in the budget, remains at the same levels. The increases and decreases in overall administrative costs broadly balance each other out, though not all of the real costs currently appear in central government's accounts. Savings are made through the abolition of Ofsted, local education authorities and examination boards and a reduction in the size of the schools ministry. Additional expenditure is needed to fund CAAT regional boards and, at a modest level, local school networks.

Who Pays?

There will be significant start-up and development costs for a period of about five years, probably peaking in the second and third year when the re-training is at its most intensive and schools temporarily require additional staffing so that practitioners can be released to train or be trained.

The funding of CAAT and its regional boards would be straightforward to achieve through a block grant reflecting CAAT's business plan. It would be helpful if the grant were designed to cover a three-year period, though governments have always been resistant to financial planning for a period longer than a year.

A big issue is how the financing of schools is best administered. Past experience suggests that the use of 'middlemen' between central government and schools only serves to increase administrative costs and the amount held back from schools by, for instance, local education authorities. The least worst solution, therefore, is probably for schools to be financed directly by government through a central agency. Governments' track record in doing this is distinctly mixed, but provided that the rules for determining the funding formula are set out simply and clearly and the operation of the agency is monitored by the finance branch of the schools ministry or organisations such as the audit commission, there is no reason in principle why this system should not work efficiently.

A precept from central government would not, however, be the only source of funding. Here I enter dragon country by proposing that school boards, within strictly applied limits, could make a charge on parents. This is, of course, heresy of the first order. Free state education has been an article of faith for well over a century. However, there are several reasons for rethinking this position. The first and the weakest is by analogy. Most people have to pay something for their 'free' health and dental care. They may not welcome paying for prescriptions but it does not stop them going to the doctor. Why should schooling be different? The second reason relates to a weakness in human nature. It is a sad fact that most people do not value what they do not have to pay for. Once they start to contribute, however modestly, they begin to insist on high quality. The third reason is economic. The vast increase in national and individual wealth since free education was introduced means that most people can now afford to pay something towards their children's education. As with the National Health Service, those who are still below the poverty line or have exceptional circumstances could be exempted from payment.

There is, however, no reason why financial support should come only from central government and parents. School boards would have the power to invite contributions from the local community and elsewhere and should have reasonable expectations that these would be forthcoming.

There are both altruistic and more self-serving reasons why local businesses and other organisations might wish to contribute to a local school, as many do already. An important feature of the joient system is the concept of partnership, and there are good reasons why the contribution of partners should be financial as well as taking other forms. Through putting money into a school, investors can expect a voice in its operation and claim a right to criticise it when necessary.

Another source of finance is from charitable institutions or well-disposed individuals, often but not necessarily part of the local community. The notion that 'charity begins at home' – or in this case at school – has rather fallen by the wayside; understandably so in face of the many world-wide problems that need our charitable support. Nevertheless, the concept of former pupils who have prospered and 'friends' of the school with spare disposable income offering financial support is something that could be extended far beyond the laudable but usually small-scale efforts of parent-teacher associations and the like. Both the independent sector schools and the universities already raise substantial sums through appeals, especially to alumni.

To counter the inevitable differences between economically advantaged and disadvantaged areas in its inhabitants' ability to contribute and in the density of businesses between urban and rural areas, altruistic contributors would be encouraged to contribute to national, regional or special interest schemes to which schools boards in impoverished areas could apply for funding. The wealthier members of the farming community, for example might contribute to a fund specifically designed to support schools situated in rural areas where farmers are not wealthy. National associations, such as that for the blind, could build up funds to support special schools and units for the partially sighted that face particular needs which the national formula for school funding does not fully meet.

Although the raising of the additional school funding, including fixing the rate of the charge on parents, would be the responsibility of school boards, they would be required by law to consult both parents and community representatives before deciding on the rate of the charge. The law would also require their accounts to be professionally audited and made easily accessible to all. Something akin to a shareholder's meeting would be held annually, open to all parents and contributing partners, in which the board would present its annual report and make provisional budget and levy proposals for the following year. The board would be legally bound to abide by any motions carried by a substantial majority of those attending or voting by proxy. Rules would need to be devised about who would be entitled to vote.

Of course, the notion of a school levy will be unpopular with parents, at least at first, but many will come to appreciate the value of having a financial stake in the success of their children's school.

Chapter 21

Fundamental and Desirable Elements in History

An opening position paper – history's low image with young people – disagreement over essential knowledge – time – evidence – causation – categories of desirable elements – links with other subjects – historical contexts for other subjects' elements

The last page of the Atlas is the only one that attempts, in part, a large-scale map of one small part of the joient system. What follows is not an attempt to draft the historical elements themselves but to provide an example of what an opening position paper might look like. This would act as a basis for subject-group discussions leading to decisions in principle before the actual drafting gets under way. I make no claim to originality in what follows. Most of the fundamental work on identifying the key skills and concepts needed in school historical learning was done by the Schools Council History Project some forty years ago. For the most part I have merely re-shaped this work to fit the joient system.

The position paper which follows (approximately two thousand words) stands as an example of how the debate might begin within the various subject groups. Undoubtedly it would lead to robust, perhaps acrimonious, debate from which would eventually emerge a first draft of what the historical segment of the national curriculum framework would look like. The rest of the process, for history and all other subjects, has already been outlined in an earlier chapter.

History as a school subject is at a disadvantage in a number of ways. Most children are concerned primarily with the present and the immediate future. As they grow older they become increasingly interested in the further future but the past remains for most of them both boring and irrelevant. They may enjoy good historical stories well told and their imaginations can be aroused by, for example, 'history days' in castles and stately homes, battle re-enactments or child-friendly museums, but they are likely to regard these as fun rather than important. Many people only discover a natural interest in history when they are well into middle age, and therefore do not as young people realise the value of history in making sense of the world around them and assisting their own personal development. History therefore has an uphill task in sparking pupils' motivation yet at the same time teaching them concepts that are central to their educational learning. Embedding historical learning within a joient offers the opportunity to overcome the problem of poor motivation and to raise pupils' awareness of how history can contribute to their knowledge and understanding of the world and to their personal, social and emotional development.

History as a discipline is based on three concepts: time, evidence and causation. All three need to figure in the fundamental elements that make up the joient curricular framework. Because all three are concepts they mainly contribute to understanding, and to a lesser extent to attitudes/actions. Although, at advanced level and beyond, effective historical learning requires a range of subject specific skills, before this stage most of the skills needed for historical learning are the general skills of language and reasoning. The only slight exception relates to the interpretation of evidence. Skills, therefore, do not figure amongst the fundamental elements. Nor does historical knowledge. This last statement will be strongly contested, especially by those for whom history is all about heritage and 'how we come to be what we are'. This is an enticing idea but fundamentally flawed and, furthermore, politically dangerous. Put any random group of people or gathering of historians in a room and ask them to come up with, say, the ten essential pieces of historical knowledge that all should know and there will be as many answers as there are people in the room. There will be a measure of agreement over certain topics, currently slavery for instance, and some that routinely figure in the top ten, such as the Holocaust. But for the most part, each individual's choice will be determined by their perception of 'what we are (and I am)' and what they perceive their heritage to be. Even the most liberal and politically correct members of the group will be hard pressed to decide which of the hundreds of worthy topics clamouring for attention should make it to the top ten. Governments, however, have a strong vested interest in pupils learning the 'national story' in ways that suit their purpose. From the earliest times to president Putin, some governments have required school history books to be re-written to glorify the present regime, legitimise its rise to power and justify its policies. It can be argued, therefore, that even in a moderate liberal democracy, such as the United Kingdom, those who decide on the history that children learn need to be armed against the dangers of governments wishing to mould the past to suit their present intentions.

This historical Tower of Babel is not just a fanciful vision. It has happened on the many occasions when historians have sat down to hammer out a common curriculum. However desirable in principle, it is impossible in practice to reach unanimous agreement on specific areas of knowledge that are essential for all. A possible compromise position would be to specify as fundamental the kinds of historical topic that must be included. These might include, for example, turning points in recent British and European history, an ancient civilisation, a period of rapid change and a particular thread of historical development, such as technological development, over a long time span. Even at this level of generality, however, there are too many types of history that might qualify for agreement to be easily reached. It seems best to accept at the outset that no single historical topic or kind of topic can be unassailably proven to be fundamental and to reserve the debate about knowledge to the later consideration of the desirable elements, where it may prove somewhat easier to agree topics that should be given priority.

Important concepts though they are, both time and evidence can be dealt with quite briefly. Identifying what is fundamental learning does not pose serious problems. Causation is a much more complex matter and distinguishing the fundamental from the desirable is more challenging.

A concern with time past is, self evidently, the defining characteristic of historical learning. Though central to the subject, the basic grammar of time is limited in scope and for the most part relatively easy to learn. The youngest pupils need to develop a basic understanding of past time in such terms as 'long, long ago', 'a long time ago', 'not long ago' and perhaps in terms of markers in their own lives – 'when I was baby', 'when I could walk', 'when I started at nursery'. As they grow older they need increasingly to develop the vocabulary of past time, the AD or Common Era (CE) dating system, the division into centuries and 'ages' such as the Stone Age or Middle Ages. By school leaving age they need to understand that dating systems are an artificial construct which can constrain understanding as well as enlighten, that other dating systems have existed in the past and continue to exist, and that certain dates carry a quasi-mystical significance, such as the Millennium and anniversaries of key events, that affects human behaviour. Through the whole period of schooling they need to develop an increasingly sophisticated understanding of the concept of anachronism, moving from recognising anachronistic facts – no motor cars, or dinosaurs, in the middle ages – to anachronistic modes of thought – science not separate from magic in the western world before the 17th century. Arguably, they will also need to have some understanding of the concepts of the 'spirit of the age' though this will be hard to define in ways specific enough to assess whether this level of conceptual understanding has been reached.

The questions such as 'how do we know?' and 'how certain can we be?' underlie all historical learning. As they grow older, pupils need to progress from an understanding that there has to be evidence for everything that we 'know' about the past to a realisation that all historical knowledge deals in degrees of probability. They also need to realise that historical evidence is subject to bias in the evidential source, to wilful or unintended misinterpretation and to conflicting versions of events. They also increasingly need to understand that some kinds of evidence are more likely to be reliable than others. In the realm of skills rather than understanding, they need to demonstrate increasing capacity to interpret different kinds of evidence, identifying bias and prejudice. In the realm of attitudes and actions, they need to develop a respect for evidence. This in turn needs to be linked to an understanding of how evidence can be deliberately misused to make a case, support a political ideology and so on through propaganda, 'spin' or the suppression of evidence. There are clear links and overlaps in this element with other disciplines: law, philosophy, politics, psychology and English literature in such works as *1984* and *Brave New World*. It is not essential, therefore, that this understanding is demonstrated wholly through historical subject matter, and an important lesson to be learnt by the oldest pupils is an appreciation that the 'rules' of historical evidence apply also to any account of human endeavour, past or present.

Causation is a shorthand word for the four, closely linked concepts of cause, consequence, change and continuity. Whilst it is possible analytically to consider these separately, it is more practical to treat them as a group. The understanding of causation starts with the realisation that everything that has happened in the past has a cause and doesn't just happen, that things that happen have consequences and that there is a chain of cause and consequence. For the youngest pupils this realisation first dawns in their own 'history'. 'The stone in the path to school made me fall over; falling over made my knee bleed and mummy had to clean it, so we were late for nursery'. As they mature, pupils start to link causal chains with change, as in the links between Early Man's use of hunting weapons, population growth and the need to move from hunter-gathering to farming. A little later still they grow to understand that causal chains can also inhibit change and promote continuity in certain circumstances. As they near the end of their schooling, they increasingly understand that causal chains are rarely if ever simple and linear but complex and varied. They appreciate that a single event can have many causes, both long and short term and of differing importance, and similarly can have many and varied consequences. Parallel to this development is pupils' increasingly sophisticated understanding of the related causal concept of motivation, progressing from a realisation that everything that people do is for a reason – they are angry, jealous, hungry etc., through the idea that people in a group may have the same or different motives for acting in the same way – to an appreciation of unconscious motivation and the complexities of events and actions resulting from a mix of physical and motivational causes.

This completes the fundamental elements of historical learning. While they are relatively few, the potential number of desirable elements is very large in terms of detailed topics for study. There is no point in engaging in endless debate about what should be in and what out – should Greeks and Romans both be included and what about Egyptians, or Mesopotamians, given the current obsession with Iraq and Iran? If some kinds of topic are not to be included amongst the fundamental elements, it is necessary to propose certain categories of historical topic and leave schools to choose particular topics from them. Drawing on the work of the Schools History Project, these topics might include: a theme studied over a long period of time; civilisations distant in time and location illustrating growth and decline; periods of rapid change, periods of massive change, periods of relative stability; the impact of outstanding historical figures; religious, cultural, social, economic, political and local community topics; recent and more distant history; British, European and World history, including a topic from every continent; historical origins of key topical or recent events and developments. Within each of these categories, a list of specific topics needs to be recommended, subject to periodic revision as current concerns change. These topic lists are, however, advisory rather than prescriptive.

Most of the desirable elements are defined in terms of knowledge and specific understanding related to particular categories of topic, for instance understanding the factors that commonly bring about the decline of civilisations. Some elements are included, not primarily to increase conceptual learning but to advance personal development. In a topic such as the 18th century Atlantic slave trade, the acquisition of factual knowledge is secondary to the main purpose of sensitising pupils to the different moralities of different eras and civilisations.

History's potential links with other subjects are many and various. A substantial proportion of elements relate to concepts shared with other subject disciplines, for example the relationship between wealth, politics and religious/cultural beliefs and their effects on the art of the Renaissance or the 'Saatchi era', or the links between topography, geology, climate, agriculture, politics, social structure and technological development in the siting of a medieval village settlement or the growth of a modern metropolis.

Some concepts that other subject groups may define as fundamental or desirable, such as the difference between power and authority in politics, can be best understood in a historical context. This approach will occasionally be useful in enhancing learning about sensitive moral or ideological issues which, if not introduced in a historical context, would be difficult for pupils to consider in a sufficiently rational and objective manner. Whilst this use of history will not figure as a formal part of the national curriculum framework, those responsible for planning joients should be encouraged to consider historical context as a possible catalyst for effective learning in certain circumstances.

Conclusion

Concluding chapters should be short and this one is no exception. Readers who have persevered thus far will have formed their own conclusions; 'visionary', 'bunkum', 'stimulating but flawed' and so on. To summarise is to imply that the earlier writing has been not been clear enough for readers to summarise for themselves.

So no summary; just an attempt to answer to two questions: 'will the joient system ever happen?' and 'if it did, would it be a success?' The perfectly logical, short but wholly unhelpful answer to both questions is 'I don't know'. Speculation about the future is just that – speculative. Answers based on an educated guess may be more illuminating. The chances of the joient system coming into being are small but not nil; the likelihood of its succeeding, if introduced, is quite good.

The proposals have little in common with the educational policies of any of the main political parties and attack some of their sacred cows such as the notion of 'choice'. For these reasons any impetus for change would have to come from the public at large and the educational establishment. The public at large, though constantly complaining about the quality of state education, tend to prefer conservative rather than radical solutions. Little support can be expected from the existing educational establishment since the proposals include the abolition of many of their roles. Those who feel that teaching by subject specialists is essential will not favour the proposals. Because many such teachers hold positions of authority in schools and elsewhere, their opposition will carry weight.

Ranged against this phalanx of Goliaths, there may, however, be some Davids with the skills to make an impact on current opinion. Within the teaching profession, there are still those who recognise the shortcomings of the present system and have a passionate, if currently subdued, desire to improve it. These proposals might just be the spark which re-kindles their passion and engenders a new grass-roots activism. In the past a handful of independent schools, or quasi-independent schools such as Telford, successfully pioneered many important innovations that have, in time, become embedded in mainstream practice. In recent decades, the independent sector's pioneering zeal has faded but these proposals might encourage a new generation of brave pioneers who would lead the way that others might eventually follow.

Though my best guess is that the joient seed will fall on stony ground, I would bet a modest sum that some features of the curricular proposals will be picked up and implemented at least in part. If these features were demonstrably successful then, in time, more of the proposals might come to be implemented more widely. They might come to be seen by politicians as sufficiently attractive to the general public and sufficiently successful to warrant inclusion in their policies. Who knows what might then develop?

But, given the chance of implementation, how likely is success? My view, based not just on hunch, but on watching teachers at work for many years, is that the chances of success are high, given two pre-conditions. The first is that the powers that be allow schools and teachers sufficient autonomy and flexibility to try out new ideas. There are some encouraging recent signs of movement in this direction. The second is that those who are in a position to try out the proposals are sufficiently inspired and confident of their rightness to persevere through the early days when they will meet with much opposition and downright hostility from some quarters. Some teachers, from at least the time of Peter Abelard onwards, have dared to take on the educational establishment. They have not always won but rarely has their struggle been without positive impact on the educational world in the long term, however reluctant the establishment has been to admit this at the time.

Ideas, like seeds, often lie dormant for long periods until the right conditions appear for them to grow and flourish. King Alfred the Great had a vision for education in the eighth century that only came to fruition in the eighteenth. My hope is that the introduction of the joient system will not have to wait quite that long!

www.ingramcontent.com/pod-product-compliance
Ingram Content Group UK Ltd.
Pitfield, Milton Keynes, MK11 3LW, UK
UKHW041436180426
11947UKWH00007B/481